AppSec Mastery

A CISO's Handbook for ISO 27001:2022 Compliance

Mohamed Fawzi Elgendi

www.fawzooz.ai

Book Title: AppSec Mastery

Author's Name: Mohammed Fawzi Elgendi

Publisher: Mohammed Fawzi Elgendi (fawzooz.ai)

Address: Al Qouz Creative Zone, Dubai, United Arab Emirates

Book Language: English

Category: Applied Sciences (Technology)

Publishing Printing & Text Permit: MC-01-013039210

ISBN: 9789948702580

Age Classification : E
"The age group suitable for the book's content has been classified and determined according to the age classification system issued by the UAE Media Council"

Printing:

Lightning Source FZC LLC, Sharjah Publishing City, United Arab Emirates

Copyright

Preface

In today's digital age, where information is the lifeblood of organizations, ensuring the security of that information has never been more critical. The evolving landscape of technology brings with it a myriad of opportunities, but also an ever-expanding array of threats. As organizations increasingly rely on complex software systems to drive their operations, the need for robust information security practices within the software development process has become paramount. This book is born out of the urgent necessity to address these challenges head-on. Over the past several years, I have had the privilege of working as a Chief Information Security Officer (CISO), where I have witnessed firsthand the transformative impact that a well-implemented Information Security Management System (ISMS) can have on an organization. My experiences have shown me that security is not just a technical requirement—it is a fundamental business enabler that protects the core assets of any organization.

The journey of integrating security into the very fabric of software development is not without its complexities. It requires a deep understanding of both security principles and the intricacies of software engineering. It demands continuous adaptation to new threats and an unwavering commitment to excellence. This book aims to provide a comprehensive guide to navigating these challenges, offering practical insights and actionable strategies for building a resilient security framework within your software development processes. Throughout the chapters of this book, you will find a blend of theoretical foundations and practical applications. We will explore the essential components of an ISMS, delve into the integration of security within DevSecOps, and examine the importance of risk management in today's dynamic threat environment. You will also find guidance on managing third-party relationships, fostering a culture of security, and staying ahead of emerging threats.

This book is intended for a wide audience, from seasoned security professionals to software developers and IT leaders who are seeking to enhance their organization's security posture. Whether you are just beginning to implement an ISMS or looking to refine your existing practices, the insights provided here will serve as a valuable resource on your journey. As you embark on this journey, remember that information security is not a one-time effort, but an ongoing process of continuous improvement. The threats we face will continue to evolve, but by fostering a culture of security, leveraging the right tools and frameworks, and committing to a proactive approach, we can safeguard our organizations against the uncertainties of the digital world.

I hope that this book will inspire you to view information security not as a hurdle, but as a critical component of your organization's success. Together, we can build a safer and more secure future for the digital age.

Table of Contents

Part1

Introduction

Chapter 1

The Importance of Information Security in Software Development

The Evolving Landscape of Information Security in Software Development

In the ever-evolving digital world, information security has transitioned from being a mere compliance checkbox to becoming a cornerstone of successful software development. As someone with over six years of experience as a Chief Information Security Officer (CISO), I have witnessed firsthand the growing importance of integrating security into every aspect of the software development lifecycle. The stakes have never been higher, with cyber threats increasing in both sophistication and frequency. This reality demands a robust, proactive approach to safeguarding the integrity, confidentiality, and availability of information.

The Role of ISO 27001:2022 in Modern Software Development

ISO 27001:2022 represents the gold standard for information security management systems (ISMS). This standard provides a systematic approach to managing sensitive company information, ensuring it remains secure. In the context of software development, ISO 27001:2022 is not just about ticking compliance boxes—it's about embedding security into the very fabric of development processes, from initial design to deployment and beyond.

In my tenure as a CISO, I have seen how organizations that prioritize security at every stage of the development lifecycle are better positioned to protect their assets, build trust with clients, and maintain a competitive edge in the marketplace. This book is a culmination of that experience, offering insights and practical guidance on implementing an ISMS tailored for the unique challenges of software development.

Why This Book?

This book is designed to be a comprehensive guide for professionals seeking to understand and implement ISO 27001:2022 within their software development practices. Whether you are a security professional, a software developer, or a business leader, this book will provide you with the tools and knowledge needed to build a secure software development environment.

Drawing on my extensive experience in information security, I will walk you through the key principles, practices, and strategies necessary to achieve and maintain compliance with ISO 27001:2022. More importantly, I will show you how to create a culture of security that goes beyond compliance—one that permeates every aspect of your organization's operations.

A Practical Approach

What sets this book apart is its practical approach. Each section is designed to not only explain the theoretical aspects of ISO 27001:2022 but also to provide actionable steps that can be implemented in real-world scenarios. From risk assessment and treatment to secure software development practices, every chapter is crafted with the practitioner in mind.

You will find detailed explanations of the processes and controls that are critical to a robust ISMS, accompanied by examples and templates that you can adapt to your own organization's needs. The goal is to equip you with the knowledge and tools to not only comply with ISO 27001:2022 but to also enhance your organization's overall security posture.

The Journey Ahead

Implementing an ISMS in a software development environment is a journey—one that requires commitment, continuous improvement, and a deep understanding of both security principles and the development process. This book is your guide on that journey, providing you with the insights and strategies needed to navigate the complexities of information security in the digital age.

As you delve into the chapters ahead, remember that security is not a destination but an ongoing process. It is about building resilience, fostering a security-first culture, and continually adapting to new challenges and threats. With the right approach, you can ensure that your software development processes are not only compliant with ISO 27001:2022 but are also robust enough to withstand the ever-changing threat landscape.

The Growing Threats in the Digital Landscape

In today's interconnected world, the digital landscape is evolving at an unprecedented pace. With this rapid evolution comes a corresponding increase in the number, sophistication, and impact of cyber threats. As organizations become more reliant on digital systems and software to drive their operations, they also become more vulnerable to a wide range of security risks. Understanding these threats is crucial for developing effective strategies to protect sensitive information and maintain the integrity of software systems.

The Rise of Cybercrime

Cybercrime has become a lucrative industry, with criminal organizations leveraging advanced technologies to exploit vulnerabilities in software and networks. The motivations behind these attacks vary, ranging from financial gain to political objectives, but the consequences are uniformly severe. Ransomware, phishing, and advanced persistent threats (APTs) are just a few examples of the tools in a cybercriminal's arsenal.

- **Ransomware:** This type of malware encrypts an organization's data, rendering it inaccessible until a ransom is paid. Ransomware attacks have surged in recent years, targeting businesses of all sizes. The impact can be devastating, leading to significant financial losses, operational disruptions, and reputational damage.
- **Phishing:** Phishing attacks, where attackers masquerade as trustworthy entities to steal sensitive information, remain a common threat. These attacks often serve as entry points for more sophisticated intrusions, such as APTs or malware installations.
- **Advanced Persistent Threats (APTs):** APTs are prolonged and targeted cyberattacks in which an intruder gains access to a network and remains undetected for an extended period. APTs are typically used to steal data or intellectual property and are often sponsored by nation-states or well-funded organizations.

The Complexity of Supply Chain Attacks

As software development increasingly relies on third-party components and open-source libraries, supply chain attacks have emerged as a significant threat. In these attacks, adversaries target vulnerabilities in third-party software that is integrated into an organization's systems. Once compromised, these components can serve as a vector for injecting malicious code, which can spread across multiple organizations that use the affected software.

Supply chain attacks are particularly insidious because they exploit the trust that organizations place in their suppliers and partners. The SolarWinds breach, one of the most notorious supply chain attacks in recent history, highlighted the potential for widespread damage when core infrastructure is compromised.

Insider Threats

Not all threats originate from external actors. Insider threats, where employees or contractors misuse their access to company systems and data, are a growing concern. These threats can be intentional, such as in cases of industrial espionage or fraud, or unintentional, stemming from negligence or a lack of security awareness.

The challenge with insider threats is that they often go undetected until significant damage has been done. Traditional security measures, such as firewalls and intrusion detection systems, are less effective against insiders who already have legitimate access to critical systems.

The Proliferation of IoT Devices

The Internet of Things (IoT) has revolutionized many industries, but it has also introduced new security challenges. IoT devices, from smart thermostats to industrial control systems, are often designed with convenience and functionality in mind, with security as a secondary consideration. As a result, many IoT devices are vulnerable to attacks that can compromise not only the devices themselves but also the broader networks to which they are connected.

The Mirai botnet attack, which harnessed thousands of compromised IoT devices to launch a massive distributed denial-of-service (DDoS) attack, is a stark reminder of the potential risks posed by insecure IoT systems.

Evolving Threat Landscape: AI and Machine Learning

The advent of artificial intelligence (AI) and machine learning (ML) is a double-edged sword in the world of cybersecurity. While these technologies offer powerful tools for detecting and mitigating threats, they also provide adversaries with new capabilities. AI-driven attacks can be more adaptive, personalized, and harder to detect. For example, AI can be used to craft more convincing phishing emails or to automate the process of finding and exploiting vulnerabilities.

Furthermore, as organizations increasingly rely on AI and ML for critical decision-making processes, these systems themselves become targets. Attacks on AI models, such as poisoning training data or exploiting biases, represent a new frontier in cybersecurity challenges.

Regulatory and Compliance Pressures

In response to the growing threat landscape, governments and regulatory bodies worldwide are imposing stricter regulations on data protection and cybersecurity. Compliance with regulations such as the General Data Protection Regulation (GDPR), Health Insurance Portability and Accountability Act (HIPAA), and the Payment Card Industry Data Security Standard (PCI DSS) has become a critical concern for organizations.

Non-compliance can result in severe penalties, legal actions, and loss of business. However, the complexity and variability of these regulations across different regions add another layer of challenge for organizations trying to maintain a strong security posture.

Conclusion

The digital landscape is fraught with ever-evolving threats that pose significant risks to organizations worldwide. From sophisticated cybercriminals and insider threats to the challenges of securing IoT devices and AI systems, the need for robust, proactive security measures has never been greater. Understanding these threats is the first step in developing an effective strategy to protect your organization's assets and ensure the security of your software development processes.

In the chapters that follow, we will explore how to address these challenges through the implementation of a comprehensive Information Security Management System (ISMS) that aligns with ISO 27001:2022. By integrating security into every aspect of your operations, you can build resilience against these threats and safeguard your organization in an increasingly hostile digital world.

Importance of Integrating Security into the Software Development Lifecycle (SDLC)

In today's digital environment, security can no longer be an afterthought in the software development process. As cyber threats grow in complexity and frequency, integrating security into the Software Development Lifecycle (SDLC) has become a necessity for any organization committed to delivering secure, reliable software products. This proactive approach ensures that security considerations are embedded in every phase of development, from initial design to deployment and beyond, rather than being retrofitted at the end of the process.

Reducing Vulnerabilities Early in the Process

One of the most compelling reasons to integrate security into the SDLC is the ability to identify and mitigate vulnerabilities early in the development process. By incorporating security practices during the initial stages of design and coding, organizations can prevent many common security flaws, such as SQL injection, cross-site scripting (XSS), and buffer overflows, from being introduced into the codebase.

Early identification of security issues is not only more effective but also more cost-efficient. Research consistently shows that the cost of fixing a vulnerability increases exponentially the later it is detected in the development process. By addressing security from the outset, organizations can reduce the time and resources required to remediate issues, avoiding the costly and potentially damaging consequences of deploying insecure software.

Ensuring Compliance with Regulatory Requirements

Many industries are subject to stringent regulatory requirements related to data protection and information security. Regulations such as GDPR, HIPAA, and PCI DSS mandate that organizations implement robust security measures to protect sensitive information. By integrating security into the SDLC, organizations can ensure that their software development processes comply with these regulations from the ground up.

Compliance is not just a legal obligation—it is a critical component of maintaining customer trust and avoiding the severe penalties associated with non-compliance. Embedding security into the SDLC ensures that security controls are not only implemented but are also documented and auditable, which is essential for demonstrating compliance during regulatory reviews and audits.

Building a Culture of Security Awareness

Integrating security into the SDLC helps foster a culture of security awareness across the entire development team. When security is treated as an integral part of the development process, rather than as an external requirement, developers, testers, and operations teams become more engaged in security practices.

This cultural shift is crucial for ensuring that everyone involved in the development process understands their role in protecting the organization's assets. Developers learn to write secure code, testers focus on identifying security flaws, and operations teams are vigilant in maintaining secure environments. This collective responsibility reduces the likelihood of security oversights and promotes a mindset where security is a shared priority.

Enhancing Product Quality and Trust

Security is a key component of overall product quality. Software that is secure by design is not only more resilient to attacks but also more reliable in terms of performance and stability. By embedding security into the SDLC, organizations can deliver higher-quality products that meet the security expectations of their customers.

In an era where data breaches and cyberattacks are headline news, customers are increasingly aware of the importance of security. Products that are built with security in mind are more likely to earn the trust of customers, leading to stronger customer relationships, reduced churn, and a competitive advantage in the marketplace.

Facilitating Continuous Improvement

Integrating security into the SDLC is not a one-time effort; it is an ongoing process that evolves as new threats emerge and technologies change. By making security an integral part of the development lifecycle, organizations create a framework for continuous improvement. Feedback loops from security testing, incident response, and user feedback can be used to refine and enhance security practices over time.

This continuous improvement approach ensures that the organization's security posture remains robust and adaptive to new challenges. It also enables the development team to learn from past experiences, improving their ability to anticipate and mitigate future security risks.

Supporting Secure DevOps (DevSecOps) Practices

The rise of DevOps has revolutionized software development by promoting collaboration between development and operations teams and emphasizing automation and continuous delivery. However, traditional DevOps practices often overlook security, leading to potential vulnerabilities in rapidly deployed code.

Integrating security into the SDLC supports the principles of DevSecOps, where security is embedded into every stage of the DevOps pipeline. This approach ensures that security checks and controls are automated and integrated into the continuous integration/continuous deployment (CI/CD) processes, enabling organizations to deliver secure software at speed and scale.

Conclusion

The importance of integrating security into the Software Development Lifecycle (SDLC) cannot be overstated. In a world where the threat landscape is constantly evolving, embedding security into every phase of development is essential for reducing vulnerabilities, ensuring compliance, building a culture of security, enhancing product quality, and supporting continuous improvement.

By making security an intrinsic part of the SDLC, organizations can not only protect their own assets but also deliver secure, trustworthy software that meets the needs and expectations of their customers. In the chapters that follow, we will explore practical strategies and best practices for achieving this integration, ensuring that security is not just an afterthought, but a fundamental component of the software development process.

Overview of ISO 27001:2022 and Its Relevance to Software Development

ISO 27001:2022 is the internationally recognized standard for managing information security. It provides a systematic approach to securing sensitive information, ensuring that organizations can effectively manage and protect their information assets. The standard outlines the requirements for establishing, implementing, maintaining, and continuously improving an Information Security Management System (ISMS).

At its core, ISO 27001:2022 is designed to help organizations safeguard the confidentiality, integrity, and availability of their information. This is achieved through a risk management process that involves identifying potential threats, assessing vulnerabilities, and implementing appropriate controls to mitigate risks.

Key Components of ISO 27001:2022

ISO 27001:2022 is structured around several key components that together form a comprehensive framework for information security management:

- **Context of the Organization:** Understanding the internal and external factors that affect the organization's ability to achieve its information security objectives.
- **Leadership:** The role of top management in driving the ISMS, establishing an information security policy, and ensuring that responsibilities are clearly defined.
- **Planning:** Identifying and addressing risks and opportunities through a structured risk assessment and treatment process.
- **Support:** Ensuring that the necessary resources, competencies, and communication processes are in place to support the ISMS.
- **Operation:** Implementing the necessary controls and processes to manage risks and achieve information security objectives.
- **Performance Evaluation:** Monitoring and measuring the effectiveness of the ISMS through regular audits, reviews, and performance assessments.
- **Improvement:** Continuously improving the ISMS by addressing nonconformities, implementing corrective actions, and adapting to changes in the threat landscape.

The Relevance of ISO 27001:2022 to Software Development

In the context of software development, ISO 27001:2022 plays a critical role in ensuring that security is integrated into every stage of the Software Development Lifecycle (SDLC). Given the increasing reliance on software in every aspect of business and society, the security of software systems is paramount. ISO 27001:2022 provides a structured approach to embedding security into software development processes, helping organizations to produce secure, compliant, and resilient software products.

Integrating Security into the SDLC

One of the most significant benefits of ISO 27001:2022 for software development is its emphasis on integrating security into the SDLC. By aligning software development practices with the requirements of ISO 27001:2022, organizations can ensure that security is not an afterthought but a fundamental aspect of the entire development process.

This integration includes:

- **Security Requirements Definition:** Identifying and documenting security requirements early in the development process, ensuring that they are aligned with business objectives and regulatory obligations.
- **Secure Design and Architecture:** Applying secure design principles, such as least privilege and defense in depth, to create robust software architectures that can withstand potential attacks.
- **Secure Coding Practices:** Ensuring that developers adhere to secure coding standards, reducing the likelihood of introducing vulnerabilities into the codebase.
- **Security Testing:** Implementing comprehensive security testing, including static and dynamic analysis, penetration testing, and vulnerability assessments, to identify and address security issues before software is deployed.

Enhancing Compliance and Risk Management

ISO 27001:2022 provides a risk-based approach to information security, which is particularly relevant in software development. By conducting regular risk assessments, organizations can identify potential threats to their software systems and implement appropriate controls to mitigate those risks.

Compliance with ISO 27001:2022 also helps organizations meet the requirements of other relevant regulations and standards, such as the General Data Protection Regulation (GDPR), the Health Insurance

Portability and Accountability Act (HIPAA), and the Payment Card Industry Data Security Standard (PCI DSS). This is particularly important for organizations that develop software for industries with stringent security and privacy requirements.

Building Customer Trust and Confidence

In an era where data breaches and cyberattacks are increasingly common, customers and stakeholders are more concerned than ever about the security of the software products they use. ISO 27001:2022 certification demonstrates an organization's commitment to maintaining high standards of information security.

For software development companies, this certification can be a key differentiator in the marketplace, helping to build trust and confidence among clients. It assures customers that the organization follows best practices in information security and is dedicated to protecting their data.

Facilitating Continuous Improvement

ISO 27001:2022 promotes a culture of continuous improvement, which is essential in the dynamic field of software development. The standard requires organizations to regularly review and update their ISMS to address new threats, vulnerabilities, and changes in the business environment.

This continuous improvement process ensures that the organization's security practices evolve alongside the development of new software technologies and methodologies. It also helps organizations stay ahead of emerging threats and maintain compliance with evolving regulations.

Conclusion

ISO 27001:2022 is not just a set of guidelines for information security—it is a comprehensive framework that, when effectively implemented, can transform the way organizations approach software development. By integrating the principles and practices of ISO 27001:2022 into the SDLC, organizations can produce secure, reliable software that meets the highest standards of information security.

In the chapters that follow, we will explore in detail how to implement ISO 27001:2022 within a software development environment, providing practical guidance and best practices for achieving and maintaining compliance. Whether you are a software developer, security professional, or business leader, understanding and applying ISO 27001:2022 is critical to safeguarding your organization’s software assets and building trust with your customers.

Chapter 2

Overview of the ISMS Manual

Brief Introduction to the Purpose and Structure of the ISMS Manual

The Information Security Management System (ISMS) manual serves as the cornerstone of an organization's commitment to protecting its information assets. In the context of software development, this manual is designed to provide a comprehensive framework for managing and safeguarding the confidentiality, integrity, and availability of information throughout the entire Software Development Lifecycle (SDLC).

The primary purpose of the ISMS manual is to:

- **Establish a Security Framework:** The manual outlines the policies, procedures, and controls necessary to protect the organization's information assets. It ensures that these security measures are integrated into all aspects of software development, from initial planning to post-deployment maintenance.
- **Ensure Compliance:** By aligning with the ISO 27001:2022 standard, the ISMS manual helps the organization meet its legal, regulatory, and contractual obligations. It provides a clear roadmap for achieving and maintaining compliance, which is particularly important in industries with stringent data protection requirements.
- **Mitigate Risks:** The manual provides a systematic approach to identifying, assessing, and treating risks related to information security. By proactively addressing potential threats and vulnerabilities, the ISMS manual helps to minimize the likelihood and impact of security incidents.
- **Support Business Continuity:** The ISMS manual includes guidelines for developing and implementing procedures that ensure the continuity of critical software development activities, even in the face of disruptions such as cyber incidents, system failures, or natural disasters.
- **Foster a Security-First Culture:** The manual promotes a culture of security awareness and responsibility across the organization. It ensures that all employees, from developers to top management, understand their roles in maintaining a secure environment and are equipped to fulfill those responsibilities.
- **Guide Continuous Improvement:** The ISMS manual is a living document that evolves alongside the organization. It provides the

framework for ongoing review and improvement of security practices, ensuring that the ISMS remains effective in the face of changing threats and technologies.

Structure of the ISMS Manual

The ISMS manual is structured to provide a clear, logical progression from understanding the organizational context to implementing and improving security controls. Each section is designed to address a specific aspect of information security management, ensuring comprehensive coverage of the organization's needs. Here is an overview of the key sections:

- **Introduction**
  - **Purpose**: Defines the objectives of the ISMS manual and its relevance to the organization.
  - **Scope**: Details the boundaries of the ISMS, including the processes, activities, and information systems it covers.
- **Context of the Organization**
  - **External and Internal Issues**: Identifies the factors that influence the organization's ability to achieve its information security objectives.
  - **Stakeholder Expectations**: Outlines the needs and expectations of stakeholders, including clients, employees, and regulators.
- **Leadership and Commitment**
  - **Information Security Policy**: Establishes the organization's overarching approach to information security.
  - **Roles and Responsibilities**: Defines the roles, responsibilities, and authorities for information security within the organization.
  - **Leadership in Software Security**: Describes how top management demonstrates its commitment to integrating security into the SDLC.
- **Planning**
  - **Risk Assessment and Treatment**: Provides the methodology for identifying, assessing, and mitigating risks to information security.
  - **Information Security Objectives**: Sets specific, measurable goals for achieving the desired security outcomes.
  - **Statement of Applicability**: Details the controls selected from ISO 27001:2022 and their relevance to the organization.
- **Support**
  - **Resources and Competence**: Ensures that the necessary resources and skills are available to implement and maintain the ISMS.

- **Training and Awareness**: Promotes security awareness and provides training to ensure all employees are equipped to contribute to information security.
- **Communication**: Establishes processes for effective communication of security policies, incidents, and other relevant information.

- **Operation**
  - **Operational Controls**: Details the specific controls and processes required to manage security risks in software development.
  - **Secure SDLC**: Describes how security is integrated into each phase of the software development lifecycle.
  - **Incident Management**: Provides guidelines for responding to security incidents, including detection, response, and recovery.
- **Performance Evaluation**
  - **Monitoring and Measurement**: Outlines the methods for assessing the effectiveness of the ISMS and identifying areas for improvement.
  - **Internal Audit**: Details the process for conducting internal audits to ensure ongoing compliance with ISO 27001:2022.
  - **Management Review**: Describes the process for top management to review the ISMS and make decisions on improvements.
- **Improvement**
  - **Nonconformity and Corrective Action**: Provides procedures for addressing nonconformities and implementing corrective actions.
  - **Continual Improvement**: Establishes a process for the ongoing enhancement of the ISMS, ensuring it adapts to new challenges and opportunities.
- **Annexes**
  - **Risk Assessment Methodology**: Detailed description of the methods used to assess risks.
  - **Information Security Controls**: A mapping of controls from Annex A of ISO 27001:2022, including those specific to software development.
  - **Glossary of Terms**: Defines key terms used throughout the ISMS manual to ensure clarity and consistency.
- **Approval and Revision History**
  - **Approval**: Records the approval of the ISMS manual by top management.
  - **Revision History**: Documents the changes made to the ISMS manual over time, ensuring transparency and traceability.

Conclusion

The ISMS manual is more than just a document—it is a strategic tool that guides the organization in implementing and maintaining a robust information security management system. By following the structure outlined above, the manual provides a clear, organized approach to managing information security, ensuring that the organization is well-equipped to protect its assets, comply with regulations, and respond to the ever-evolving threat landscape. As we delve into the specific sections of the ISMS manual in this book, you will gain a deeper understanding of how each component contributes to building a secure software development environment.

Key Objectives of the ISMS Manual

The Information Security Management System (ISMS) manual serves as the foundational document that guides an organization's approach to information security, particularly within the context of software development. The manual is designed with several key objectives in mind, each aimed at ensuring the protection of the organization's information assets and the secure delivery of its software products. These objectives are critical for maintaining compliance with ISO 27001:2022 and for fostering a culture of security across the organization.

Ensuring Compliance with Regulatory and Industry Standards

One of the primary objectives of the ISMS manual is to ensure that the organization complies with all relevant legal, regulatory, and industry-specific standards. In today's highly regulated environment, compliance is not optional—it is a necessity. The manual provides a clear framework for meeting the requirements of ISO 27001:2022, as well as other regulations such as GDPR, HIPAA, and PCI DSS.

- **Legal Compliance:** The manual ensures that the organization adheres to all applicable laws governing data protection, privacy, and information security, reducing the risk of legal penalties and reputational damage.
- **Regulatory Compliance:** By aligning with standards such as ISO 27001:2022, the manual helps the organization meet its regulatory obligations, demonstrating a commitment to maintaining high standards of information security.
- **Industry Standards:** The manual incorporates best practices from across the industry, ensuring that the organization's security practices are in line with those of its peers and competitors.

Mitigating Risks to Information Assets

Another critical objective of the ISMS manual is to provide a structured approach to identifying, assessing, and mitigating risks to the organization's information assets. In the context of software development, these assets include source code, customer data, intellectual property, and the development environment itself.

- **Risk Identification:** The manual outlines processes for systematically identifying potential risks, including threats from cyberattacks, insider threats, and vulnerabilities in third-party components.
- **Risk Assessment:** It provides a methodology for evaluating the likelihood and impact of identified risks, helping the organization prioritize its security efforts.
- **Risk Mitigation:** The manual details the controls and procedures that should be implemented to reduce the likelihood of security incidents and minimize their impact when they do occur.

Protecting the Confidentiality, Integrity, and Availability of Information

The core of any ISMS is the protection of the organization's information assets. The ISMS manual is designed to safeguard the confidentiality, integrity, and availability (CIA) of information, which are the three pillars of information security.

- **Confidentiality:** The manual ensures that sensitive information is only accessible to authorized individuals, protecting it from unauthorized access or disclosure.
- **Integrity:** It provides guidelines for maintaining the accuracy and completeness of information, preventing unauthorized modifications that could compromise data quality.
- **Availability:** The manual outlines procedures to ensure that information and systems are accessible when needed, supporting the organization's operational needs and business continuity.

Integrating Security into the Software Development Lifecycle (SDLC)

For software development organizations, one of the most important objectives of the ISMS manual is to embed security into every phase of the Software Development Lifecycle (SDLC). This integration ensures that security is not an afterthought but a fundamental aspect of the development process.

- **Security by Design:** The manual promotes the adoption of secure design principles from the earliest stages of development, reducing the risk of vulnerabilities being introduced into the software.
- **Secure Coding Practices:** It provides guidelines for secure coding, ensuring that developers follow best practices to prevent common security flaws such as SQL injection and cross-site scripting (XSS).
- **Comprehensive Testing:** The manual emphasizes the importance of thorough security testing, including static and dynamic analysis, to identify and address vulnerabilities before software is deployed.

Supporting Business Continuity and Incident Response

The ISMS manual plays a crucial role in ensuring that the organization is prepared to respond effectively to security incidents and maintain business continuity in the face of disruptions.

- **Incident Response Planning:** The manual provides a framework for detecting, responding to, and recovering from security incidents, minimizing their impact on the organization's operations.
- **Disaster Recovery:** It includes guidelines for disaster recovery planning, ensuring that critical systems and information can be restored quickly in the event of a major disruption.
- **Business Continuity:** The manual supports the development of business continuity plans that ensure the organization can continue to operate even during adverse conditions, such as cyberattacks or natural disasters.

Fostering a Security-First Culture

The ISMS manual is not just a technical document—it is also a tool for fostering a culture of security awareness and responsibility throughout the organization. By clearly defining roles, responsibilities, and expectations, the manual helps to ensure that every employee understands their role in protecting the organization's information assets.

- **Security Awareness:** The manual outlines training and awareness programs designed to educate employees about the importance of information security and their responsibilities under the ISMS.
- **Roles and Responsibilities:** It clearly defines the roles and responsibilities of all employees, from top management to developers, ensuring that security is a shared responsibility across the organization.
- **Continuous Improvement:** The manual promotes a culture of continuous improvement, encouraging employees to regularly review and enhance security practices in response to new threats and challenges.

Driving Continuous Improvement in Information Security

Finally, the ISMS manual is designed to be a living document that evolves with the organization. One of its key objectives is to drive continuous improvement in information security, ensuring that the ISMS remains effective in the face of changing technologies, threats, and business needs.

- **Regular Reviews:** The manual includes processes for regularly reviewing and updating the ISMS, incorporating feedback from audits, incidents, and emerging best practices.

- **Adaptability:** It provides a flexible framework that can be adapted to meet the organization's evolving security needs, ensuring that the ISMS remains relevant and effective over time.
- **Innovation:** The manual encourages the adoption of new security technologies and practices, helping the organization stay ahead of emerging threats and maintain a strong security posture.

Conclusion

The ISMS manual is a critical tool for any organization committed to protecting its information assets and maintaining a robust security posture. By clearly defining the objectives outlined above, the manual provides a comprehensive framework for managing information security, ensuring compliance, mitigating risks, and fostering a culture of continuous improvement. In the chapters that follow, we will explore how to achieve these objectives in practice, providing you with the knowledge and tools needed to implement an effective ISMS within your software development environment.

Part 2

Building the Foundation

Chapter 1

Understanding the ISO 27001:2022 Standard

Detailed Explanation of ISO 27001:2022

ISO 27001:2022 is the latest iteration of the internationally recognized standard for establishing, implementing, maintaining, and continually improving an Information Security Management System (ISMS). The standard is designed to help organizations of all sizes and industries systematically manage and protect their sensitive information. By following ISO 27001:2022, organizations can ensure that their information assets are secured against evolving threats while complying with regulatory and contractual obligations.

What is ISO 27001:2022?

ISO 27001:2022 is a structured framework that outlines the best practices for managing information security risks. It provides organizations with a set of requirements for building an ISMS, which is a comprehensive system of policies, procedures, and controls designed to manage risks to information security and ensure the confidentiality, integrity, and availability of information.

The 2022 version of the standard introduces updates and refinements to address the changing landscape of information security, particularly in response to emerging threats, technological advancements, and evolving regulatory requirements. The standard is part of the ISO/IEC 27000 family of standards, which collectively cover a broad spectrum of information security management practices.

Key Components of ISO 27001:2022

ISO 27001:2022 is organized into several key sections, each of which addresses a critical aspect of information security management. The standard is structured around the Plan-Do-Check-Act (PDCA) cycle, which promotes a continuous improvement approach to managing information security.

Context of the Organization

This section emphasizes the importance of understanding the internal and external factors that can affect the organization's ability to achieve its information security objectives. It involves:

- **Understanding the Organization and Its Context:** Identifying the internal and external issues that are relevant to the ISMS and that can influence its effectiveness.
- **Understanding the Needs and Expectations of Interested Parties:** Identifying stakeholders, including customers, employees, regulators, and partners, and understanding their needs and expectations regarding information security.
- **Determining the Scope of the ISMS:** Defining the boundaries and applicability of the ISMS, including the processes, systems, and information assets that it covers.
- **Establishing the ISMS:** Formally establishing the ISMS in accordance with the requirements of ISO 27001:2022, ensuring it is aligned with the organization's strategic objectives.

Leadership and Commitment

Top management plays a critical role in the successful implementation and operation of the ISMS. This section outlines the responsibilities of leadership in driving the ISMS forward:

- **Leadership and Commitment:** Ensuring that top management demonstrates leadership and commitment by actively supporting the ISMS, allocating resources, and promoting a culture of information security.
- **Information Security Policy:** Developing, implementing, and maintaining an information security policy that sets the direction and principles for the ISMS.
- **Roles, Responsibilities, and Authorities:** Defining and assigning roles, responsibilities, and authorities related to information security, ensuring that these are communicated across the organization.

Planning

Planning is essential for identifying and addressing risks and opportunities related to information security. This section covers:

- **Actions to Address Risks and Opportunities:** Establishing a process for identifying and assessing risks and opportunities that could affect the ISMS, and implementing actions to address them.
- **Information Security Objectives and Planning to Achieve Them:** Setting specific, measurable objectives for information security and developing plans to achieve these objectives.
- **Planning of Changes:** Ensuring that any changes to the ISMS are planned and implemented in a controlled manner, taking into account the potential impact on information security.

Support

The effectiveness of the ISMS depends on having the right resources, competencies, and communication processes in place. This section addresses:

- **Resources:** Ensuring that the necessary resources (financial, human, technical) are available to support the ISMS.
- **Competence:** Determining and ensuring that employees have the necessary competencies to perform their information security roles effectively.
- **Awareness:** Ensuring that all employees are aware of the information security policy, their roles in the ISMS, and the implications of not conforming to ISMS requirements.
- **Communication:** Establishing processes for internal and external communication related to the ISMS, ensuring that relevant information is communicated effectively.
- **Documented Information:** Managing documented information required by the ISMS, including policies, procedures, and records, to ensure that it is accurate, up-to-date, and accessible.

Operation

This section focuses on the implementation of the ISMS and the controls necessary to manage information security risks:

- **Operational Planning and Control:** Planning, implementing, and controlling the processes needed to meet the requirements of the ISMS and achieve its objectives.
- **Risk Assessment and Risk Treatment:** Continuously assessing information security risks and implementing appropriate controls to mitigate them. This includes developing a Statement of Applicability (SoA) that lists the controls selected from Annex A and justifies their inclusion or exclusion.
- **Managing Outsourced Processes:** Ensuring that outsourced processes that affect information security are controlled and monitored in accordance with the ISMS.

Performance Evaluation

To ensure that the ISMS remains effective, it is essential to monitor, measure, analyze, and evaluate its performance. This section covers:

- **Monitoring, Measurement, Analysis, and Evaluation:** Establishing processes for monitoring and measuring the performance of the ISMS, including the effectiveness of controls and the achievement of information security objectives.

- **Internal Audit:** Conducting regular internal audits to assess whether the ISMS conforms to ISO 27001:2022 and is effectively implemented and maintained.
- **Management Review:** Ensuring that top management regularly reviews the ISMS to assess its performance and identify opportunities for improvement.

Improvement

The ISMS must be continually improved to adapt to changes in the threat landscape, business environment, and technological advancements. This section includes:

- **Nonconformity and Corrective Action:** Establishing processes for identifying nonconformities, determining their causes, and implementing corrective actions to prevent recurrence.
- **Continual Improvement:** Promoting a culture of continuous improvement, ensuring that the ISMS evolves over time to address new challenges and opportunities.

Annex A: Reference Control Objectives and Controls

Annex A of ISO 27001:2022 provides a comprehensive list of security controls that organizations can implement to address identified risks. These controls are organized into several domains, including:

- **Information Security Policies:** Controls related to the management of information security policies.
- **Organization of Information Security:** Controls related to the management and governance of information security within the organization.
- **Human Resource Security:** Controls to ensure that employees, contractors, and third parties are aware of their information security responsibilities.
- **Asset Management:** Controls related to the management of information assets, including classification, handling, and protection.
- **Access Control:** Controls to ensure that access to information is restricted to authorized users.
- **Cryptography:** Controls related to the use of cryptographic techniques to protect information.
- **Physical and Environmental Security:** Controls to protect the physical security of information assets.

- **Operations Security:** Controls related to the secure management of IT operations and infrastructure.
- **Communications Security:** Controls to protect the security of communications and data transfers.
- **System Acquisition, Development, and Maintenance:** Controls to ensure that information security is integrated into the software development lifecycle.
- **Supplier Relationships:** Controls to manage the security risks associated with third-party suppliers.
- **Information Security Incident Management:** Controls to ensure that security incidents are identified, reported, and managed effectively.
- **Information Security Aspects of Business Continuity Management:** Controls to ensure the continuity of information security during business disruptions.
- **Compliance:** Controls to ensure compliance with legal, regulatory, and contractual requirements.

Each control in Annex A is mapped to specific risks identified during the risk assessment process, and organizations can select the controls that are most relevant to their needs.

The Certification Process

Achieving ISO 27001:2022 certification involves several steps:

- **Gap Analysis:** Conducting an initial assessment to identify gaps between the organization's current practices and the requirements of ISO 27001:2022.
- **Implementation:** Developing and implementing the ISMS based on the requirements of the standard, including the necessary policies, procedures, and controls.
- **Internal Audit:** Conducting an internal audit to assess the effectiveness of the ISMS and identify any areas for improvement.
- **Certification Audit:** Engaging an accredited certification body to conduct an external audit. The certification audit is typically conducted in two stages:
    - **Stage 1 Audit:** A preliminary review of the ISMS documentation and readiness for certification.
    - **Stage 2 Audit:** A detailed assessment of the implementation and effectiveness of the ISMS.
- **Certification:** If the organization passes the certification audit, it is awarded ISO 27001:2022 certification, which is valid for three years, subject to annual surveillance audits.

Benefits of ISO 27001:2022

Implementing ISO 27001:2022 provides numerous benefits to organizations, including:

- **Enhanced Security Posture:** A structured approach to managing information security risks, reducing the likelihood of security incidents.
- **Regulatory Compliance:** Demonstrates compliance with legal, regulatory, and contractual requirements, reducing the risk of fines and penalties.
- **Customer Trust:** Builds trust with customers and stakeholders by demonstrating a commitment to protecting their information.
- **Competitive Advantage:** Differentiates the organization in the marketplace, providing a competitive edge in industries where security is a critical concern.
- **Continuous Improvement:** Promotes a culture of continuous improvement, ensuring that the organization remains resilient in the face of evolving threats.

Conclusion

ISO 27001:2022 is a comprehensive standard that provides organizations with a robust framework for managing information security risks. By implementing the requirements of the standard, organizations can ensure the confidentiality, integrity, and availability of their information assets, while also meeting regulatory obligations and building trust with stakeholders. In the context of software development, ISO 27001:2022 is particularly valuable for embedding security into every stage of the development lifecycle, ensuring that software products are secure, reliable, and compliant with industry standards.

How ISO 27001:2022 Applies to Software Development

ISO 27001:2022 is a powerful framework for managing information security, and its principles are particularly relevant to the software development process. As software development increasingly becomes a core function in many organizations, the need to secure the entire Software Development Lifecycle (SDLC) has never been greater. By applying ISO 27001:2022 to software development, organizations can ensure that security is embedded into every phase of the development process, from initial concept to deployment and beyond.

Embedding Security in the Software Development Lifecycle (SDLC)

ISO 27001:2022 provides a structured approach to integrating security into each phase of the SDLC. This integration helps to prevent vulnerabilities from being introduced into the software, ensures compliance with security standards, and protects sensitive data throughout the development process.

- **Requirements Gathering:** During the initial phase of the SDLC, ISO 27001:2022 guides the identification and documentation of security requirements. This ensures that security considerations are aligned with business objectives and regulatory requirements from the outset.
- **Design:** In the design phase, ISO 27001:2022 encourages the application of secure design principles, such as least privilege and defense in depth. Threat modeling is also used to identify potential security risks and design appropriate controls.
- **Development:** ISO 27001:2022 promotes the use of secure coding practices, ensuring that developers follow industry best practices to avoid common vulnerabilities like SQL injection and cross-site scripting (XSS). The standard also supports the use of secure development environments, version control, and access management.
- **Testing:** Security testing is a critical component of the ISO 27001:2022 framework. The standard emphasizes the importance of integrating static and dynamic security testing, penetration testing, and vulnerability assessments into the testing phase of the SDLC. This helps to identify and address security issues before the software is released.

- **Deployment:** ISO 27001:2022 ensures that security controls are maintained during the deployment phase. This includes secure configuration management, access controls, and the use of automated deployment tools to enforce security settings.
- **Maintenance and Monitoring:** After deployment, ISO 27001:2022 supports ongoing security monitoring, vulnerability management, and incident response. This ensures that the software remains secure throughout its operational life, even as new threats emerge.

Risk Management in Software Development

One of the core principles of ISO 27001:2022 is risk management, which is especially relevant in the context of software development. The standard provides a framework for identifying, assessing, and mitigating risks that could impact the security of software products.

- **Risk Identification:** In software development, risks can arise from various sources, including vulnerabilities in the code, third-party components, or misconfigurations in the development environment. ISO 27001:2022 guides the systematic identification of these risks, ensuring that they are documented and understood.
- **Risk Assessment:** Once risks are identified, ISO 27001:2022 provides methodologies for assessing the likelihood and impact of these risks. This helps organizations prioritize their security efforts, focusing on the most critical risks.
- **Risk Treatment:** ISO 27001:2022 outlines strategies for treating risks, including mitigating risks through the implementation of security controls, transferring risks (e.g., through insurance or outsourcing), avoiding risks by altering development processes, and accepting risks when they fall within the organization's risk tolerance.
- **Ongoing Risk Management:** ISO 27001:2022 promotes continuous risk management, ensuring that risks are regularly reviewed and that the effectiveness of controls is monitored throughout the SDLC. This proactive approach helps to address new risks as they emerge.

Compliance with Legal and Regulatory Requirements

Software development often involves handling sensitive data, whether it's customer information, intellectual property, or financial data. ISO 27001:2022 helps organizations ensure that their software development processes comply with relevant legal and regulatory requirements, such as GDPR, HIPAA, and PCI DSS.

- **Data Protection:** ISO 27001:2022 requires that security controls be implemented to protect sensitive data throughout the SDLC. This includes encryption, access controls, and data anonymization techniques to ensure compliance with data protection laws.

- **Auditability:** The standard promotes the creation and maintenance of detailed documentation and audit trails, which are essential for demonstrating compliance during audits and regulatory reviews.
- **Third-Party Compliance:** Many software development projects involve third-party components or services. ISO 27001:2022 helps organizations manage these relationships by ensuring that third-party suppliers adhere to the same security standards and compliance requirements.

Enhancing Product Quality and Customer Trust

ISO 27001:2022 is not just about protecting information—it's also about ensuring the quality and reliability of software products. By embedding security into the SDLC, organizations can produce software that is not only secure but also robust and trustworthy.

- **Product Quality:** Secure software is typically higher quality software. By following ISO 27001:2022, organizations can avoid many common pitfalls that lead to security vulnerabilities, resulting in more stable and reliable software products.
- **Customer Trust:** ISO 27001:2022 certification is a mark of trust. It signals to customers that the organization is committed to the highest standards of information security. This can be a key differentiator in a competitive marketplace, helping to build long-term customer relationships.
- **Reputation Management:** By preventing security incidents and ensuring compliance, ISO 27001:2022 helps organizations protect their reputation. In the event of a security breach, the standard provides guidelines for effective incident response, minimizing damage to the organization's reputation.

Supporting Secure DevOps (DevSecOps) Practices

The rise of DevOps has transformed software development by emphasizing collaboration between development and operations teams and promoting rapid, continuous delivery. ISO 27001:2022 supports the principles of DevSecOps, where security is integrated into every stage of the DevOps pipeline.

- **Automated Security Testing:** ISO 27001:2022 encourages the use of automated security tests within the CI/CD pipeline, ensuring that every code change is tested for security issues before it is deployed.

- **Security as Code:** The standard supports the concept of "security as code," where security policies and controls are codified and automatically enforced throughout the SDLC. This ensures that security is consistently applied, even in fast-paced development environments.
- **Collaboration:** ISO 27001:2022 promotes cross-functional collaboration, ensuring that development, operations, and security teams work together to achieve common security objectives. This aligns with the DevSecOps philosophy of integrating security into the culture of the organization.

Continuous Improvement and Adaptability

The dynamic nature of software development means that the threat landscape is always evolving. ISO 27001:2022 provides a framework for continuous improvement, ensuring that security practices evolve in response to new challenges.

- **Feedback Loops:** ISO 27001:2022 encourages the usc of feedback loops to continuously improve security practices. This includes learning from security incidents, audits, and testing results, and using this knowledge to enhance the ISMS and SDLC processes.
- **Adaptability:** The standard's emphasis on regular reviews and updates ensures that the ISMS remains adaptable to changes in technology, business processes, and the threat environment. This is particularly important in software development, where innovation and agility are key to success.

Conclusion

ISO 27001:2022 is a critical standard for organizations involved in software development. By applying the principles and practices outlined in the standard, organizations can ensure that security is embedded into every phase of the SDLC, from concept to deployment. This not only helps to protect sensitive information and ensure compliance with legal and regulatory requirements but also enhances the overall quality and reliability of software products. In the fast-paced world of software development, where security threats are constantly evolving, ISO 27001:2022 provides a structured, proactive approach to managing risks and protecting information assets. By adopting this standard, organizations can build secure, trustworthy software that meets the needs of their customers and stakeholders, while also maintaining a competitive edge in the marketplace.

Key Terms and Concepts in ISO 27001:2022

Understanding the key terms and concepts in ISO 27001:2022 is essential for effectively implementing and maintaining an Information Security Management System (ISMS). These concepts form the foundation of the standard and guide how organizations approach information security within the context of their operations, particularly in software development.

Information Security Management System (ISMS)

An ISMS is a systematic approach to managing sensitive company information so that it remains secure. It includes people, processes, and IT systems by applying a risk management process. The ISMS is designed to protect the confidentiality, integrity, and availability of information by managing the risks associated with information security.

- **Confidentiality:** Ensures that information is accessible only to those authorized to have access.
- **Integrity:** Safeguards the accuracy and completeness of information and processing methods.
- **Availability:** Ensures that authorized users have access to information and associated assets when required.

Context of the Organization

This concept involves understanding the internal and external factors that can affect the ISMS's ability to achieve its objectives. The context of the organization helps in determining the scope of the ISMS and identifying the relevant stakeholders and their expectations.

- **Internal Context:** Includes the organization’s culture, structure, roles, and relationships that impact information security.
- **External Context:** Encompasses external influences like legal, regulatory, technological, and social factors that can affect the ISMS.

Risk Management

Risk management is the process of identifying, assessing, and controlling threats to an organization's capital and earnings. In the context of ISO

27001:2022, it involves a continuous cycle of risk assessment, risk treatment, and risk monitoring to protect information assets.

- **Risk Assessment:** The process of identifying risks to information security, analyzing the potential impact of these risks, and determining their likelihood.
- **Risk Treatment:** Actions taken to mitigate, transfer, accept, or avoid risks. This may involve implementing security controls to reduce the risk to an acceptable level.
- **Risk Appetite:** The level of risk that an organization is willing to accept in pursuit of its objectives.

Information Security Policy

An information security policy is a set of rules and guidelines that governs how an organization manages and protects its information assets. The policy is a critical component of the ISMS and must be approved by top management to ensure that it aligns with the organization's objectives.

- **Policy Statement:** A high-level declaration of the organization's commitment to information security.
- **Supporting Policies:** Detailed policies that address specific areas such as access control, data protection, and incident management.

Controls

Controls are measures that are put in place to mitigate risks to information security. In ISO 27001:2022, controls are selected based on the results of the risk assessment and are documented in the Statement of Applicability (SoA).

- **Preventive Controls:** Aim to prevent security incidents from occurring (e.g., encryption, access controls).
- **Detective Controls:** Designed to identify and detect security incidents (e.g., intrusion detection systems, monitoring).
- **Corrective Controls:** Focus on responding to and recovering from security incidents (e.g., backup and recovery processes).

Statement of Applicability (SoA)

The Statement of Applicability is a document that lists all the controls that are applicable to the organization based on its risk assessment. It includes justifications for including or excluding each control from Annex A of ISO 27001:2022 and is a key document in the certification process.

- **Annex A Controls:** A set of 93 security controls grouped into 14 domains, ranging from information security policies to compliance with legal requirements.

- **Control Objectives:** Specific goals that each control aims to achieve in reducing information security risks.

Continual Improvement

Continual improvement is a fundamental principle of ISO 27001:2022. It involves the ongoing effort to enhance the ISMS and ensure that it adapts to new threats, changes in the business environment, and advancements in technology.

Plan-Do-Check-Act (PDCA) Cycle: A four-step model used to drive continual improvement in the ISMS:

- **Plan:** Establish the ISMS, policies, and objectives.
- **Do:** Implement and operate the ISMS.
- **Check:** Monitor and review the ISMS against the requirements and objectives.
- **Act:** Maintain and improve the ISMS based on the results of the monitoring and review process.

Leadership and Commitment

ISO 27001:2022 emphasizes the role of top management in driving the ISMS. Leadership and commitment are crucial for ensuring that information security is integrated into the organization's culture and that sufficient resources are allocated to the ISMS.

- **Top Management:** The group of people who direct and control an organization at the highest level. They are responsible for ensuring that the ISMS aligns with the organization's strategic direction.
- **Information Security Roles and Responsibilities:** Clearly defined roles and responsibilities for information security that are communicated across the organization.

Interested Parties

Interested parties are individuals or groups that have an interest in the organization's information security performance. These can include customers, employees, regulators, suppliers, and shareholders.

- **Stakeholder Needs and Expectations:** Understanding what interested parties expect from the ISMS and how these expectations influence the organization's approach to information security.

Incident Management

Incident management involves the identification, management, and resolution of security incidents to minimize their impact on the organization. ISO 27001:2022 provides guidance on how to handle incidents effectively.

- **Security Incident:** Any event that could lead to unauthorized access, use, disclosure, disruption, modification, or destruction of information.
- **Incident Response Plan:** A documented plan that outlines the steps to take when a security incident occurs, including roles and responsibilities, communication protocols, and recovery procedures.

Documented Information

Documented information is a key concept in ISO 27001:2022, referring to all the documents and records required to demonstrate the effective implementation of the ISMS.

- **Policies and Procedures:** Formal documents that describe how the ISMS is implemented and operated.
- **Records:** Evidence that activities related to the ISMS have been performed as required.

Internal Audit

An internal audit is a process of evaluating the effectiveness of the ISMS by assessing its conformity with ISO 27001:2022 and identifying areas for improvement. It is an essential part of the "Check" phase in the PDCA cycle.

- **Audit Criteria:** The set of policies, procedures, and standards against which the ISMS is audited.
- **Audit Findings:** The results of the audit, including any nonconformities and opportunities for improvement.

Nonconformity and Corrective Action

Nonconformities are instances where the ISMS does not meet the requirements of ISO 27001:2022 or the organization's own policies and procedures. Corrective actions are steps taken to address these nonconformities and prevent their recurrence.

- **Nonconformity:** A deviation from a specified requirement.
- **Corrective Action:** Measures taken to eliminate the cause of a nonconformity and prevent its recurrence.

Business Continuity Management

Business continuity management involves ensuring that the organization can continue to operate in the event of a significant disruption, such as a cyberattack, natural disaster, or system failure. ISO 27001:2022 integrates information security into broader business continuity planning.

- **Business Impact Analysis (BIA):** A process for assessing the potential impact of a disruption on the organization's operations.
- **Disaster Recovery Plan:** A documented plan for recovering critical systems and data following a significant disruption.

Access Control

Access control is a critical component of information security, involving the management of who has access to information and systems. ISO 27001:2022 provides guidance on implementing access controls to ensure that only authorized individuals can access sensitive information.

- **Authentication:** The process of verifying the identity of a user, device, or other entity before granting access.
- **Authorization:** The process of granting or denying specific access rights to a user, device, or other entity.

Conclusion

These key terms and concepts form the backbone of ISO 27001:2022 and are essential for anyone involved in the implementation and management of an ISMS. By understanding and applying these concepts, organizations can effectively protect their information assets, comply with regulatory requirements, and build a robust security culture within their software development processes.

Chapter 2
Establishing the Context

Defining the Scope of ISMS in a Software Development Environment

Defining the scope of an Information Security Management System (ISMS) is a critical step in implementing ISO 27001:2022 within a software development environment. The scope outlines the boundaries of the ISMS and determines which aspects of the organization's operations, processes, and assets will be covered by the information security controls and policies. A well-defined scope ensures that the ISMS is focused, effective, and aligned with the organization's business objectives and regulatory requirements.

Understanding the Organizational Context

The first step in defining the scope of the ISMS is to understand the organizational context in which the software development activities take place. This involves considering both internal and external factors that influence information security.

- **Internal Context:** This includes the organizational structure, culture, roles, and responsibilities related to software development. It also encompasses the technologies used, the types of software being developed, and the existing security policies and procedures.
- **External Context:** This involves understanding the regulatory environment, customer requirements, industry standards, and market pressures that impact the organization's approach to information security in software development.

Identifying Relevant Information Assets

In a software development environment, information assets can include a wide range of resources, each of which must be protected by the ISMS. These assets typically include:

- **Source Code:** The codebase of software applications, which is often the most critical asset in a software development environment.
- **Development Tools:** Integrated development environments (IDEs), version control systems, and other tools used in the software development process.
- **Intellectual Property:** Patents, proprietary algorithms, and design documents that are valuable to the organization.

- **Customer Data:** Any personal or sensitive data that is used, processed, or stored during the development of software applications.
- **Development and Testing Environments:** Servers, virtual machines, and other infrastructure used to develop, test, and deploy software.
- **Third-Party Components:** Open-source libraries, APIs, and other third-party software components integrated into the developed software.

Determining the Scope Boundaries

The scope of the ISMS must clearly define the boundaries within which the ISMS will operate. This includes specifying the physical, logical, and organizational boundaries.

- **Physical Boundaries:** The physical locations where software development activities take place, such as offices, data centers, and remote work environments. It also includes physical devices, such as servers and workstations, used in the development process.
- **Logical Boundaries:** The IT infrastructure, networks, and systems involved in software development. This includes both on-premises and cloud environments where development, testing, and deployment occur.
- **Organizational Boundaries:** The departments, teams, and personnel involved in the software development process. It also covers third-party vendors, contractors, and partners who have access to the development environment or the codebase.

Aligning with Business Objectives

The ISMS scope must align with the organization's overall business objectives and strategy. For a software development company, this often means focusing on protecting intellectual property, ensuring the security of customer data, and complying with relevant regulations.

- **Business Goals:** Understanding how information security supports the organization's goals, such as maintaining customer trust, ensuring compliance, and protecting competitive advantages.
- **Regulatory Requirements:** Identifying any legal, regulatory, or contractual obligations that apply to the software being developed. This might include data protection laws (such as GDPR), industry standards (such as PCI DSS), and customer-specific security requirements.

Including Relevant Processes and Activities

The scope of the ISMS should encompass all relevant processes and activities that impact information security within the software development lifecycle (SDLC).

- **SDLC Phases:** The scope should cover all phases of the SDLC, including requirements gathering, design, development, testing, deployment, and maintenance. Each phase has specific security requirements that must be addressed by the ISMS.
- **Supporting Activities:** In addition to core development activities, the scope may include supporting activities such as project management, quality assurance, and incident management, all of which play a role in maintaining information security.

Addressing Risks and Threats

The scope of the ISMS should be designed to address the specific risks and threats faced by the organization in its software development activities.

- **Risk Assessment:** Conducting a risk assessment helps identify the most significant threats to information security within the development environment. The results of this assessment will influence the scope by highlighting the areas where security controls are most needed.
- **Threat Landscape:** Understanding the current threat landscape, including common vulnerabilities in software development (such as insecure coding practices, insider threats, and supply chain risks), helps ensure that the ISMS scope is comprehensive.

Documenting the Scope

Once the scope has been defined, it must be documented clearly and concisely. The scope document should include:

- **Scope Statement:** A brief description of the scope, including the physical, logical, and organizational boundaries.
- **Inclusions and Exclusions:** A list of what is included and excluded from the ISMS, along with justifications for any exclusions. This ensures that the scope is both focused and relevant.
- **Rationale:** An explanation of how the scope aligns with the organization's business objectives, regulatory requirements, and risk profile.

Communicating the Scope

Finally, it is essential to communicate the scope of the ISMS to all relevant stakeholders, including management, development teams, and third-party partners. Clear communication ensures that everyone understands the boundaries of the ISMS and their roles in maintaining information security within those boundaries.

- **Internal Communication:** Ensuring that all employees involved in software development are aware of the ISMS scope and understand how it affects their work.
- **External Communication:** Communicating the scope to external parties, such as clients and auditors, to demonstrate the organization's commitment to information security.

Conclusion

Defining the scope of the ISMS in a software development environment is a crucial step in implementing ISO 27001:2022. The scope must be carefully considered to ensure that it covers all relevant aspects of the organization's operations, addresses key risks and threats, and aligns with business objectives. By establishing a clear and well-documented scope, the organization can ensure that its ISMS is effective in protecting information assets and supporting the secure development of software products.

External and Internal Issues Influencing Information Security

In the context of ISO 27001:2022, understanding the external and internal issues that influence information security is crucial for the effective implementation and operation of an Information Security Management System (ISMS). These issues shape the organization's risk landscape and determine the controls and processes necessary to protect its information assets. For a software development environment, these factors are particularly significant, as they directly impact the security of the software being developed, the development process itself, and the data handled by the organization.

External Issues Influencing Information Security

External issues encompass the factors outside the organization that can impact its information security. These issues are often beyond the organization's direct control but must be considered to develop a robust ISMS.

Regulatory and Legal Requirements

- **Data Protection Laws:** Regulations such as the General Data Protection Regulation (GDPR), California Consumer Privacy Act (CCPA), and Health Insurance Portability and Accountability Act (HIPAA) impose strict requirements on how organizations handle personal data. Non-compliance can lead to significant fines and reputational damage.
- **Industry Standards:** Standards such as the Payment Card Industry Data Security Standard (PCI DSS) apply to organizations that handle credit card data. Adherence to these standards is essential for maintaining customer trust and avoiding penalties.
- **Contractual Obligations:** Contracts with clients, partners, and suppliers may include specific information security requirements that must be met. Failing to comply with these obligations can result in legal action and loss of business.

Cyber Threat Landscape

- **Emerging Threats:** The ever-evolving nature of cyber threats, such as ransomware, phishing attacks, and advanced persistent threats (APTs), requires organizations to continuously adapt their security measures. Software development organizations are often targeted due to the high value of intellectual property and customer data they handle.
- **Global Cybercrime Trends:** The rise of organized cybercrime, state-sponsored attacks, and the use of artificial intelligence (AI) by attackers has increased the complexity and frequency of cyberattacks. Organizations must stay informed about these trends to protect themselves effectively.

Technological Advancements

- **Cloud Computing:** The widespread adoption of cloud services introduces new security challenges related to data protection, access control, and shared responsibility. Organizations must ensure that their cloud providers adhere to stringent security standards.
- **Internet of Things (IoT):** The proliferation of IoT devices in development environments can introduce vulnerabilities, especially if these devices are not secured properly. This includes both consumer-grade devices and specialized hardware used in development and testing.
- **Software Supply Chain:** The use of third-party libraries, open-source components, and external APIs in software development can introduce vulnerabilities into the codebase. Organizations must carefully vet these components and monitor for security updates.

Market and Economic Conditions

- **Competitive Pressure:** In a competitive market, there may be pressure to accelerate development timelines, which can lead to shortcuts in security practices. Balancing speed with security is a critical challenge for software development organizations.
- **Economic Downturns:** Economic challenges can lead to budget constraints, which may result in reduced investment in information security. This can increase the risk of security breaches if critical controls are not maintained.

Geopolitical Factors

- **Cross-Border Data Transfer:** Organizations that operate globally or handle data from multiple jurisdictions must navigate complex

regulations related to data transfer, such as data localization laws and international data transfer restrictions.
- **Political Instability:** Political instability in certain regions can lead to increased risks, such as state-sponsored cyberattacks or disruptions to the supply chain. Organizations must assess the geopolitical risks associated with their operations.

Internal Issues Influencing Information Security

Internal issues refer to factors within the organization that can affect its ability to manage information security effectively. These issues are within the organization's control and can be addressed through internal policies, processes, and culture.

Organizational Structure and Culture
- **Security Culture:** The organization's overall approach to security, including the level of awareness and commitment among employees, significantly influences the effectiveness of the ISMS. A strong security culture promotes proactive risk management and adherence to security policies.
- **Leadership Commitment:** The degree of support and involvement from top management in driving the ISMS is crucial. Without strong leadership, security initiatives may lack the necessary resources and strategic alignment.
- **Role Definition:** Clearly defined roles and responsibilities for information security help ensure accountability and effective implementation of security measures. Ambiguity in roles can lead to gaps in security coverage.

Human Resources
- **Staff Competency:** The knowledge and skills of employees, particularly in secure coding practices, threat detection, and incident response, directly impact the organization's ability to protect its information assets. Ongoing training and development are essential to maintain competency.
- **Insider Threats:** Employees, contractors, or partners with legitimate access to sensitive information can pose a significant risk if they misuse their access, either intentionally or unintentionally. Effective access control and monitoring are critical to mitigating this risk.
- **Employee Turnover:** High turnover rates can lead to a loss of institutional knowledge and potentially weaken the organization's

security posture. It's important to have robust onboarding and offboarding processes to manage access to information assets.

Technology and Infrastructure

- **IT Infrastructure:** The security of the organization's IT infrastructure, including servers, networks, and endpoints, is fundamental to protecting information assets. Regular updates, patch management, and network segmentation are essential practices.
- **Development Environment:** The security of development tools, version control systems, and testing environments must be ensured to prevent unauthorized access or modification of the codebase. This includes both on-premises and cloud-based environments.
- **Data Management:** How the organization handles data, including data storage, backup, and encryption practices, influences its ability to protect sensitive information. Proper data classification and protection measures are necessary.

Processes and Procedures

- **Software Development Lifecycle (SDLC):** The maturity and security of the organization's SDLC processes directly impact the security of the software it produces. Secure coding practices, code reviews, and security testing must be integral parts of the SDLC.
- **Incident Response:** The organization's ability to respond quickly and effectively to security incidents is a key determinant of its overall security posture. This requires well-defined and practiced incident response plans.
- **Change Management:** Effective change management processes ensure that changes to systems, applications, and infrastructure are reviewed for security implications before implementation. Poor change management can introduce vulnerabilities.

Financial Resources

- **Budget Allocation:** The amount of financial resources allocated to information security affects the organization's ability to implement and maintain necessary controls, conduct regular audits, and invest in training and technology.
- **Cost-Benefit Analysis:** Organizations must balance the cost of implementing security controls with the potential risks they mitigate. This analysis influences decisions on which controls to prioritize.

Conclusion

Both external and internal issues play a critical role in shaping an organization's information security strategy. By understanding these issues, organizations can tailor their ISMS to address specific risks and challenges relevant to their software development environment. This holistic approach ensures that the ISMS is robust, effective, and capable of adapting to the dynamic nature of both the internal and external environments in which the organization operates.

Stakeholder Engagement and Aligning ISMS with Business Strategy

Effective implementation of an Information Security Management System (ISMS) requires aligning information security practices with the organization's broader business strategy and actively engaging stakeholders throughout the process. By integrating the ISMS with business objectives and ensuring that stakeholders are involved and informed, organizations can create a security-first culture that supports both operational efficiency and long-term success.

Importance of Stakeholder Engagement

Stakeholders are individuals or groups that have an interest in or are affected by the organization's information security practices. Engaging stakeholders is crucial for several reasons:

- **Understanding Expectations:** Stakeholders, including customers, employees, partners, and regulators, have specific expectations regarding information security. Understanding these expectations helps ensure that the ISMS meets the needs of all relevant parties.
- **Gaining Support and Commitment:** Active engagement with stakeholders helps build support for the ISMS across the organization. This is particularly important for securing the necessary resources and commitment from top management and other key personnel.
- **Improving Communication:** Effective communication with stakeholders fosters transparency and trust. It ensures that stakeholders are aware of the organization's security policies, the role they play in maintaining security, and how their actions contribute to the overall security posture.
- **Enhancing Compliance:** Engaging with regulators and other external stakeholders helps ensure that the ISMS complies with legal and regulatory requirements. It also facilitates smoother audits and reduces the risk of non-compliance penalties.

Identifying and Categorizing Stakeholders

The first step in stakeholder engagement is identifying all relevant stakeholders and categorizing them based on their level of influence and interest in the ISMS.

Internal Stakeholders:

- **Top Management:** Responsible for setting the strategic direction of the ISMS and ensuring it aligns with business objectives.
- **Employees:** All staff members play a role in information security, from developers to administrative staff, and must be engaged through training and awareness programs.
- **IT and Security Teams:** These teams are directly involved in implementing and managing the ISMS and are critical to its success.
- **Project Managers:** Responsible for overseeing software development projects and ensuring that security practices are integrated into the SDLC.

External Stakeholders:

- **Customers:** They expect the organization to protect their data and maintain confidentiality, integrity, and availability.
- **Regulators:** Authorities that enforce compliance with legal and regulatory requirements, such as data protection laws.
- **Suppliers and Partners:** Organizations that provide services, products, or components that are integrated into the organization's software development process.
- **Investors:** Interested in the organization's risk management practices and their impact on financial performance.

Engaging Stakeholders in the ISMS Process

Once stakeholders are identified, the next step is to actively engage them in the ISMS process. This involves regular communication, consultation, and collaboration to ensure that their needs and expectations are addressed.

Consultation and Feedback:

- **Surveys and Interviews:** Conduct surveys and interviews with key stakeholders to gather feedback on their information security concerns and expectations.
- **Workshops and Meetings:** Hold regular workshops and meetings with stakeholders to discuss the ISMS, gather input, and build consensus on security initiatives.
- **Steering Committees:** Establish steering committees that include representatives from different stakeholder groups to provide ongoing guidance and oversight of the ISMS.

Education and Awareness:

- **Training Programs:** Develop targeted training programs to educate employees and other internal stakeholders about the ISMS, their roles in maintaining security, and best practices for information security.
- **Awareness Campaigns:** Run awareness campaigns that highlight the importance of information security and the organization's commitment to protecting information assets.

Ongoing Communication:

- **Regular Updates:** Provide stakeholders with regular updates on the status of the ISMS, including progress on key initiatives, audit results, and any changes to security policies or procedures.
- **Incident Reporting:** Establish clear channels for reporting security incidents and communicating with stakeholders about incident response and resolution.

Aligning ISMS with Business Strategy

To maximize the effectiveness of the ISMS, it must be aligned with the organization's overall business strategy. This alignment ensures that information security supports the organization's strategic goals and adds value rather than being seen as a separate or secondary concern.

Integrating Security into Business Objectives:

- **Strategic Alignment:** Ensure that the objectives of the ISMS are aligned with the organization's strategic goals, such as enhancing customer trust, protecting intellectual property, or ensuring compliance with regulations.
- **Balanced Scorecard:** Use tools like the Balanced Scorecard to integrate information security metrics into the organization's performance management system, linking security performance to business outcomes.

Supporting Business Growth:

- **Innovation and Security:** Ensure that the ISMS supports innovation by enabling the secure development and deployment of new products and services. This may involve adopting secure DevOps practices or integrating security into the SDLC.
- **Market Differentiation:** Leverage ISO 27001:2022 certification as a differentiator in the marketplace, demonstrating to customers and partners that the organization is committed to maintaining the highest standards of information security.

Risk Management and Business Continuity:

- **Risk-Based Decision Making:** Align the ISMS with the organization's risk management framework, ensuring that security risks are assessed and managed in the context of broader business risks.
- **Business Continuity Planning:** Integrate the ISMS with business continuity planning to ensure that the organization can continue operating during and after a security incident or disruption.

Resource Allocation:

- **Investment in Security:** Ensure that resources are allocated to the ISMS based on the organization's strategic priorities and risk profile. This includes investing in security technologies, personnel, and training.
- **Cost-Benefit Analysis:** Perform cost-benefit analyses to justify investments in security controls and demonstrate their value to the organization.

Monitoring and Reviewing ISMS Alignment

Alignment between the ISMS and business strategy is not a one-time task—it requires ongoing monitoring and review to ensure that the ISMS remains relevant and effective as business objectives evolve.

Performance Metrics:

- **Key Performance Indicators (KPIs):** Develop KPIs to measure the effectiveness of the ISMS in supporting business objectives. These might include metrics related to incident response times, compliance rates, or the number of security breaches prevented.
- **Regular Reporting:** Report on ISMS performance to top management and other key stakeholders, highlighting how information security initiatives are contributing to the achievement of business goals.

Continuous Improvement:

- **Regular Reviews:** Conduct regular reviews of the ISMS to ensure it remains aligned with the organization's business strategy. This includes reviewing the scope, policies, and controls of the ISMS in light of changes in the business environment.
- **Adaptation and Flexibility:** Be prepared to adapt the ISMS to meet new business challenges, such as entering new markets, adopting new technologies, or responding to emerging threats.

Conclusion

Stakeholder engagement and aligning the ISMS with business strategy are essential components of a successful information security program. By involving stakeholders in the ISMS process and ensuring that information security practices are integrated with the organization’s strategic goals, organizations can create a security-first culture that supports business growth, innovation, and resilience. Continuous engagement, communication, and alignment are key to maintaining an effective ISMS that not only protects information assets but also adds value to the organization as a whole.

Chapter 3

Leadership and Commitment

Role of Leadership in Driving Security Culture

Leadership plays a pivotal role in establishing and driving a security culture within an organization. In the context of ISO 27001:2022, leadership commitment is a critical factor for the successful implementation and ongoing effectiveness of an Information Security Management System (ISMS). Strong leadership helps ensure that security is embedded into every aspect of the organization's operations, fostering a culture where security is seen not just as a technical concern but as a shared responsibility across all levels of the organization.

Setting the Strategic Direction for Security

One of the primary responsibilities of leadership is to set the strategic direction for information security within the organization. This involves aligning the goals of the ISMS with the overall business strategy and ensuring that security becomes a fundamental part of the organization's vision and objectives.

- **Defining Security Objectives:** Leadership must establish clear, measurable security objectives that are aligned with the organization's broader business goals. These objectives should be integrated into the ISMS to ensure that security initiatives directly support business priorities, such as protecting intellectual property, ensuring customer trust, or maintaining compliance with regulations.
- **Communicating the Security Vision:** Leaders must communicate the organization's security vision and objectives to all employees, creating a shared understanding of why security is important and how it contributes to the organization's success. This communication helps to build a unified approach to security across all departments and functions.

Demonstrating Commitment to Security

Leadership commitment is one of the core principles of ISO 27001:2022. To drive a strong security culture, leaders must go beyond simply endorsing security initiatives—they must demonstrate their active involvement and commitment to maintaining a secure environment.

- **Leading by Example:** Leaders should model security-conscious behavior by following security policies, participating in security training, and taking an active role in security initiatives. When employees see leadership taking security seriously, they are more likely to adopt a security-first mindset.
- **Allocating Resources:** Leadership must ensure that adequate financial, technological, and human resources are allocated to support the ISMS. This includes investing in security technologies, hiring qualified security professionals, and providing ongoing security training for employees.
- **Participating in Security Oversight:** Top management should be directly involved in overseeing the implementation and effectiveness of the ISMS. This may include participating in regular management reviews, monitoring security performance metrics, and making decisions based on risk assessments.

Establishing Accountability and Roles

A key element of driving a security culture is establishing clear roles and responsibilities for information security throughout the organization. Leadership must ensure that everyone understands their role in maintaining security and is held accountable for their actions.

- **Defining Roles and Responsibilities:** Leadership should define and document information security roles at all levels of the organization, from executive leadership to individual contributors. This includes assigning responsibility for specific security controls, policies, and procedures, and ensuring that roles are communicated clearly.
- **Appointing a Security Champion:** Leadership may appoint a Chief Information Security Officer (CISO) or a dedicated security team to lead the organization's security efforts. These individuals or teams are responsible for driving security initiatives, conducting risk assessments, and managing the ISMS.
- **Encouraging Cross-Functional Collaboration:** Security is not the responsibility of just one team—it must be integrated across all functions, including IT, HR, legal, and operations. Leadership should encourage cross-functional collaboration to ensure that security considerations are incorporated into all business processes.

Promoting a Security-First Mindset

One of the most important roles of leadership is fostering a security-first mindset across the organization. This involves creating an environment where employees understand the importance of security, are aware of potential risks, and are proactive in safeguarding information assets.

- **Security Awareness and Training:** Leadership must ensure that all employees receive regular training on security policies, best practices, and emerging threats. This helps employees understand their role in protecting the organization and equips them with the knowledge to identify and mitigate security risks.
- **Encouraging Security Ownership:** Employees should be empowered to take ownership of security in their daily activities. Leadership can promote this by encouraging employees to report security incidents, participate in security audits, and contribute to the continuous improvement of security practices.
- **Recognizing and Rewarding Security Efforts:** Leadership should recognize and reward individuals or teams that contribute to strengthening the organization's security posture. This could include acknowledging employees who identify potential vulnerabilities, contribute to security projects, or demonstrate exceptional adherence to security protocols.

Integrating Security into Business Processes

Leadership plays a crucial role in ensuring that security is integrated into the organization's business processes and not treated as an afterthought. Security must be embedded into all aspects of the business, including strategic planning, product development, and daily operations.

- **Secure Development Practices:** For organizations involved in software development, leadership must ensure that security is embedded into the Software Development Lifecycle (SDLC). This includes secure coding practices, threat modeling, and regular security testing.
- **Risk-Based Decision Making:** Leadership must adopt a risk-based approach to decision-making, ensuring that security risks are considered when making business decisions. This involves conducting regular risk assessments and ensuring that controls are in place to mitigate identified risks.
- **Continuous Monitoring and Improvement:** Leadership should promote a culture of continuous improvement, where the ISMS is regularly reviewed and updated to reflect changes in the threat landscape, business objectives, and technological advancements.

Supporting Incident Response and Crisis Management

When security incidents occur, strong leadership is essential for an effective response. Leadership must ensure that the organization is prepared to manage security incidents and has the necessary resources and processes in place to minimize the impact of such incidents.

- **Establishing Incident Response Plans:** Leadership must ensure that comprehensive incident response plans are developed, communicated, and regularly tested. These plans should outline the steps to take in the event of a security breach, including communication protocols, roles and responsibilities, and recovery procedures.
- **Supporting Crisis Management:** In the event of a major security incident, leadership must take a visible role in managing the crisis. This includes communicating with stakeholders, coordinating the response effort, and ensuring that recovery actions are implemented quickly and effectively.
- **Post-Incident Reviews:** Leadership should promote the practice of conducting post-incident reviews to identify lessons learned and implement improvements to prevent similar incidents in the future. This demonstrates a commitment to continuous improvement and helps strengthen the organization's security posture.

Aligning Security with Business Strategy

Leadership must ensure that information security initiatives are aligned with the organization's broader business strategy. This alignment ensures that security supports business objectives rather than being seen as a separate or siloed function.

- **Balancing Security and Innovation:** Leadership must strike a balance between security and innovation. This involves promoting a culture where security is seen as an enabler of innovation rather than a barrier. For example, adopting secure DevOps practices (DevSecOps) can help integrate security into fast-paced development environments.
- **Driving Competitive Advantage:** Leadership can position information security as a competitive advantage by highlighting the organization's commitment to security and using ISO 27001:2022 certification as a differentiator in the marketplace. This can help build customer trust and improve market positioning.
- **Ensuring Regulatory Compliance:** Leadership must ensure that the ISMS aligns with legal and regulatory requirements, such as data protection laws (GDPR, HIPAA) and industry standards (PCI DSS).

This helps the organization avoid legal penalties and maintain compliance with contractual obligations.

Conclusion

The role of leadership in driving a security culture is paramount to the success of an ISMS and the overall security posture of an organization. By setting the strategic direction, demonstrating commitment, fostering a security-first mindset, and integrating security into business processes, leaders create an environment where security is prioritized and embedded in every aspect of the organization's operations. Through strong leadership, organizations can build a resilient security culture that not only protects information assets but also supports business growth and innovation.

Establishing an Information Security Policy

An Information Security Policy is a critical component of an organization's Information Security Management System (ISMS). It serves as the foundation for all security-related activities within the organization and provides clear guidelines on how information assets should be managed, protected, and used. Establishing a comprehensive and effective Information Security Policy is essential for aligning security practices with the organization's business objectives, regulatory requirements, and risk management strategies.

Purpose of the Information Security Policy

The primary purpose of an Information Security Policy is to establish the organization's commitment to protecting its information assets. The policy provides a framework for managing and safeguarding sensitive information, ensuring that it remains confidential, integral, and available to authorized users.

- **Defining Security Objectives:** The policy should clearly state the organization's security objectives, such as protecting customer data, maintaining compliance with regulations, and ensuring business continuity. These objectives should align with the organization's overall business goals.
- **Setting Expectations:** The policy sets expectations for how employees, contractors, and other stakeholders should handle and protect information. It establishes the roles and responsibilities of individuals at all levels of the organization in maintaining security.
- **Guiding Security Practices:** The policy provides high-level guidance on the security practices that the organization will implement, such as access control, data encryption, incident response, and risk management. It serves as the foundation for more detailed procedures and controls.

Key Components of an Information Security Policy

An effective Information Security Policy typically includes several key components that address different aspects of information security within the organization:

- **Policy Statement:** A high-level declaration of the organization's commitment to information security. The policy statement should emphasize the importance of protecting information assets and outline the organization's approach to achieving this goal.
- **Scope:** The scope section defines the boundaries of the policy, specifying which information assets, systems, and processes are covered. It should also identify the individuals or groups responsible for implementing and adhering to the policy.
- **Roles and Responsibilities:** This section outlines the roles and responsibilities of key stakeholders, including top management, IT and security teams, employees, and third-party contractors. It should clarify who is responsible for specific security tasks, such as risk assessments, incident response, and security awareness training.
- **Security Principles:** The policy should articulate the fundamental security principles that guide the organization's approach to information security. These principles may include confidentiality, integrity, availability, accountability, and compliance.
- **Risk Management:** This section should describe the organization's approach to managing information security risks. It should outline the process for identifying, assessing, and mitigating risks, and specify how risk management activities are integrated into the ISMS.
- **Access Control:** The policy should provide guidelines for controlling access to information and systems. This includes defining who is authorized to access specific information, how access is granted and revoked, and the use of authentication and authorization mechanisms.
- **Data Protection:** This section should outline the measures the organization takes to protect data, both at rest and in transit. It should address data classification, encryption, data retention, and disposal practices.
- **Incident Response:** The policy should establish procedures for detecting, reporting, and responding to security incidents. It should specify the roles and responsibilities of the incident response team and outline the steps to be taken in the event of a security breach.
- **Compliance and Legal Obligations:** The policy should ensure that the organization complies with all relevant legal, regulatory, and contractual requirements related to information security. It should specify the standards and regulations the organization adheres to, such as ISO 27001, GDPR, HIPAA, and PCI DSS.
- **Monitoring and Review:** The policy should describe how the organization will monitor and review its information security practices

to ensure they remain effective. This includes regular audits, management reviews, and continuous improvement activities.

- **Policy Enforcement:** This section should outline the consequences of non-compliance with the policy, including disciplinary actions for employees who violate security protocols. It should also describe the process for reporting and addressing policy violations.

Developing the Information Security Policy

Developing an Information Security Policy involves a collaborative process that engages stakeholders across the organization. This ensures that the policy is comprehensive, relevant, and aligned with the organization's needs.

- **Stakeholder Involvement:** Engage key stakeholders, including top management, IT and security teams, legal advisors, and department heads, in the development of the policy. Their input is crucial for ensuring that the policy addresses all relevant areas of information security.
- **Risk Assessment:** Conduct a thorough risk assessment to identify the key risks facing the organization. The findings of this assessment should inform the development of the policy, ensuring that it addresses the most significant threats to information security.
- **Alignment with Business Objectives:** Ensure that the policy is aligned with the organization's business objectives and supports its strategic goals. The policy should be designed to protect information assets while enabling the organization to achieve its business outcomes.
- **Compliance Requirements:** Consider the legal and regulatory requirements that apply to the organization. The policy must ensure compliance with relevant laws and standards, such as data protection regulations and industry-specific requirements.
- **Drafting the Policy:** Draft the policy in clear, concise language that is accessible to all employees. Avoid technical jargon and ensure that the policy is understandable to non-technical staff members.
- **Review and Approval:** Once the policy is drafted, it should be reviewed by key stakeholders and legal advisors to ensure it is comprehensive and compliant with relevant regulations. The final policy should be approved by top management.

Communicating the Information Security Policy

Once the Information Security Policy is established, it is essential to communicate it effectively across the organization. Clear communication ensures that all employees understand the policy and their role in maintaining information security.

- **Policy Distribution:** Distribute the policy to all employees, contractors, and relevant third parties. This can be done through email, intranet postings, or hard copies. Ensure that everyone has access to the policy and understands where to find it.
- **Training and Awareness:** Develop training programs to educate employees about the Information Security Policy and their responsibilities under it. Regular security awareness training should reinforce the key principles of the policy and highlight best practices.
- **Acknowledgment of Receipt:** Require employees to acknowledge that they have received, read, and understood the Information Security Policy. This can be done through a signed acknowledgment form or an electronic confirmation.
- **Ongoing Communication:** Keep the policy visible and top-of-mind by incorporating it into regular communications, such as newsletters, team meetings, and security bulletins. Highlight key sections of the policy and update employees on any changes or revisions.

Reviewing and Updating the Information Security Policy

The Information Security Policy should not be a static document; it must evolve with the organization and the changing threat landscape. Regular review and updating of the policy ensure that it remains relevant and effective.

- **Scheduled Reviews:** Establish a regular review schedule, typically annually or whenever there is a significant change in the organization's operations, technology, or regulatory environment. This ensures that the policy remains aligned with current risks and business objectives.
- **Continuous Improvement:** Incorporate feedback from audits, security incidents, and employee feedback into the policy review process. This allows the organization to address any gaps or weaknesses in the policy and continuously improve its security posture.
- **Version Control:** Maintain version control of the Information Security Policy, documenting any changes or updates. Ensure that all employees are informed of any revisions and understand the implications for their responsibilities.

Conclusion

Establishing an Information Security Policy is a foundational step in building a robust Information Security Management System (ISMS). The policy sets the direction for all security activities within the organization, providing clear guidance on how information assets should be protected. By involving key stakeholders in the development process, aligning the policy with business objectives, and ensuring effective communication and regular updates, organizations can create a strong security culture that supports the protection of their information assets and compliance with regulatory requirements.

Assigning Roles and Responsibilities in Information Security

Assigning clear roles and responsibilities is a crucial step in establishing an effective Information Security Management System (ISMS) under ISO 27001:2022. Clearly defined roles ensure that all aspects of information security are managed efficiently and that accountability is established across the organization. This structured approach helps in fostering a security-conscious culture where every employee understands their role in protecting the organization's information assets.

Importance of Defining Roles and Responsibilities

The success of an ISMS depends on the active participation of all employees, from top management to individual contributors. Clearly defined roles and responsibilities ensure that:

- **Accountability is Established:** Each person knows what they are responsible for, which helps prevent overlaps or gaps in security coverage.
- **Security Policies are Enforced:** With designated roles, policies and procedures are more likely to be followed, reducing the risk of non-compliance.
- **Efficient Incident Response:** In the event of a security incident, having predefined roles allows for a swift and organized response.
- **Continuous Improvement is Facilitated:** Assigned roles help ensure that ongoing monitoring, reviews, and updates to the ISMS are consistently executed.

Key Roles and Responsibilities in Information Security

Several key roles must be assigned within the organization to ensure comprehensive coverage of all aspects of information security. These roles can be categorized into three main groups: leadership roles, operational roles, and supporting roles.

Leadership Roles

- **Chief Information Security Officer (CISO):**
    - **Responsibility:** The CISO is typically the highest-ranking individual responsible for the overall information security strategy,

governance, and risk management within the organization. The CISO reports directly to senior management and ensures that security aligns with business objectives.
    - **Duties:** Developing and maintaining the ISMS, leading security initiatives, overseeing risk assessments, and ensuring compliance with legal and regulatory requirements.
- **Top Management:**
    - **Responsibility:** Senior executives and top management are responsible for endorsing the ISMS, ensuring it is aligned with the organization's strategic goals, and providing the necessary resources for its implementation and maintenance.
    - **Duties:** Approving the Information Security Policy, reviewing ISMS performance, and making decisions on resource allocation and risk management.
- **Information Security Steering Committee:**
    - **Responsibility:** This committee, often chaired by the CISO, includes representatives from various departments and functions. It is responsible for providing oversight and direction for the ISMS.
    - **Duties:** Reviewing security initiatives, approving security policies and procedures, and ensuring cross-functional alignment on security matters.

Operational Roles
- **Information Security Manager:**
    - **Responsibility:** The Information Security Manager is responsible for the day-to-day management and operation of the ISMS. This role typically reports to the CISO and focuses on implementing security policies and procedures.
    - **Duties:** Managing security controls, coordinating security training, conducting audits, and monitoring security incidents.
- **IT Security Team:**
    - **Responsibility:** The IT Security Team is responsible for implementing and maintaining technical security controls within the organization's IT infrastructure.
    - **Duties:** Managing firewalls, intrusion detection systems, encryption technologies, access controls, and conducting vulnerability assessments and penetration testing.
- **Data Protection Officer (DPO):**
    - **Responsibility:** The DPO is specifically tasked with overseeing data protection strategies and ensuring compliance with data privacy laws such as GDPR.

  - **Duties:** Monitoring data processing activities, advising on data protection impact assessments, and serving as the point of contact for regulatory authorities.
- **Incident Response Team:**
  - **Responsibility:** This team is responsible for managing the organization's response to security incidents, including detection, containment, eradication, recovery, and post-incident analysis.
  - **Duties:** Coordinating incident response activities, communicating with stakeholders during incidents, and documenting incidents for future learning.

Supporting Roles

- **Department Heads and Managers:**
  - **Responsibility:** Managers at various levels are responsible for ensuring that their teams adhere to the organization's security policies and practices.
  - **Duties:** Promoting security awareness within their teams, ensuring compliance with security policies, and reporting security incidents to the appropriate channels.
- **Human Resources (HR):**
  - **Responsibility:** HR plays a key role in embedding security into the organization's culture and processes, particularly in relation to onboarding, training, and offboarding employees.
  - **Duties:** Conducting background checks, coordinating security awareness training, and ensuring that access rights are updated as employees change roles or leave the organization.
- **Legal and Compliance:**
  - **Responsibility:** The legal and compliance teams ensure that the organization's ISMS complies with applicable laws, regulations, and contractual obligations.
  - **Duties:** Advising on legal requirements related to information security, reviewing contracts for security clauses, and managing compliance with industry standards.
- **Employees (General Staff):**
  - **Responsibility:** Every employee has a role to play in maintaining the organization's information security, from following security policies to reporting suspicious activities.
  - **Duties:** Adhering to security policies, protecting passwords and sensitive data, and participating in security training programs.

Third-Party and Vendor Roles

- **Third-Party Vendors and Contractors:**
  - **Responsibility:** Vendors and contractors who have access to the organization's information or systems must comply with the organization's security policies.
  - **Duties:** Implementing agreed-upon security controls, adhering to contractual security requirements, and reporting any security incidents that may affect the organization.

Implementing and Communicating Roles and Responsibilities

Once roles and responsibilities are defined, it is important to communicate them clearly to all relevant parties and ensure that they are implemented effectively.

- **Documentation:** Clearly document all roles and responsibilities in the ISMS documentation, such as the Information Security Policy, procedures, and job descriptions. This ensures that everyone knows their security-related duties.
- **Training:** Provide targeted training to individuals based on their roles. For example, IT staff might receive technical training on security controls, while general staff receive training on data protection and phishing prevention.
- **Awareness Programs:** Implement security awareness programs that reinforce the importance of security roles and responsibilities. Regular reminders, workshops, and newsletters can help keep security top-of-mind for all employees.
- **Accountability:** Establish mechanisms for holding individuals accountable for their security responsibilities. This could include performance evaluations, regular audits, and clear consequences for non-compliance.
- **Ongoing Review:** Regularly review and update roles and responsibilities to reflect changes in the organization, technology, and the threat landscape. This ensures that the ISMS remains relevant and effective.

Monitoring and Reviewing Responsibilities

To ensure that the assigned roles and responsibilities are being effectively carried out, regular monitoring and review are essential.

- **Internal Audits:** Conduct regular internal audits to assess how well roles and responsibilities are being fulfilled. Audits can help identify gaps or areas where additional training or resources may be needed.

- **Management Reviews:** Top management should regularly review the performance of the ISMS, including an assessment of how roles and responsibilities are being executed. This can inform decisions about adjustments or improvements.
- **Feedback Loops:** Create feedback mechanisms that allow employees to report issues or suggest improvements related to their security responsibilities. This encourages continuous improvement and helps address challenges promptly.

Conclusion

Assigning clear roles and responsibilities is a foundational element of an effective ISMS. By defining who is responsible for what, organizations can ensure that all aspects of information security are managed efficiently, risks are mitigated, and security policies are enforced. This structured approach not only supports compliance with ISO 27001:2022 but also fosters a culture of accountability and shared responsibility, where every member of the organization plays a part in protecting information assets.

PART 3

Strategic Planning

Chapter 4

Risk Assessment and Treatment

Methodology for Risk Assessment in Software Development

Risk assessment is a critical component of the Information Security Management System (ISMS) under ISO 27001:2022, particularly in the context of software development. The goal of a risk assessment is to identify, evaluate, and prioritize risks associated with the software development lifecycle (SDLC) and implement appropriate controls to mitigate those risks. A systematic approach to risk assessment helps ensure that security is integrated into every phase of software development, from design to deployment and maintenance.

Establishing the Context

Before conducting a risk assessment, it is essential to establish the context within which the assessment will be conducted. This involves understanding the scope of the software development activities, the regulatory environment, and the organization's business objectives.

- **Scope Definition:** Clearly define the boundaries of the risk assessment, including the specific software projects, development environments, and information assets that will be assessed. This includes identifying the systems, applications, data, and processes involved in the SDLC.
- **Stakeholder Identification:** Identify the stakeholders who have an interest in the risk assessment process, including developers, project managers, IT security teams, customers, and regulatory bodies.
- **Objective Setting:** Define the objectives of the risk assessment. These objectives should align with the organization's broader security and business goals, such as protecting intellectual property, ensuring compliance, and maintaining the availability of critical systems.

Identifying Risks

The next step in the risk assessment process is to identify potential risks that could impact the security, integrity, and availability of the software being developed. Risk identification should be comprehensive and consider both internal and external threats.

- **Threat Modeling:** Use threat modeling techniques to identify potential threats to the software at each stage of the SDLC. Threat modeling involves understanding how an attacker could compromise the software and what the potential impact of such an attack would be.
- **Vulnerability Analysis:** Identify vulnerabilities in the software development process, including insecure coding practices, inadequate access controls, and weaknesses in the development environment. Vulnerabilities can also exist in third-party components and libraries used in the software.
- **Asset Identification:** Identify the information assets involved in the software development process, such as source code, development tools, customer data, and intellectual property. Understanding the value of these assets helps prioritize risks.
- **Human Factors:** Consider risks associated with human factors, such as developer error, insider threats, and lack of security awareness among development teams.

Analyzing Risks

Once risks have been identified, the next step is to analyze them to determine their potential impact and likelihood. This analysis helps prioritize risks and informs decisions about which risks require the most attention.

- **Risk Likelihood:** Assess the likelihood of each identified risk occurring. This involves evaluating the probability that a particular threat will exploit a vulnerability in the software or development process. Factors to consider include the sophistication of potential attackers, the attractiveness of the target, and historical data on similar incidents.
- **Risk Impact:** Evaluate the potential impact of each risk on the organization's operations, reputation, and financial standing. The impact assessment should consider the consequences of data breaches, service disruptions, loss of intellectual property, and regulatory non-compliance.
- **Risk Rating:** Combine the likelihood and impact assessments to assign a risk rating to each identified risk. This can be done using a risk matrix, which categorizes risks as low, medium, high, or critical based on their combined score.
- **Qualitative vs. Quantitative Analysis:** Risk analysis can be qualitative (based on expert judgment and scenarios) or quantitative (based on numerical data and probabilistic models). The choice depends on the organization's needs and the availability of data.

Evaluating Risks

After analyzing the risks, the next step is to evaluate them to determine which risks are acceptable and which require mitigation. This step involves making decisions about risk treatment based on the organization's risk appetite and tolerance.

- **Risk Tolerance:** Define the organization's risk tolerance—the level of risk that the organization is willing to accept in pursuit of its objectives. Risks that exceed this threshold must be treated, while those within tolerance may be accepted.
- **Prioritization:** Prioritize risks based on their rating. High and critical risks should be addressed first, as they pose the greatest threat to the organization. Lower-rated risks may be monitored over time or treated with less intensive controls.
- **Cost-Benefit Analysis:** Conduct a cost-benefit analysis to evaluate the costs of implementing security controls against the potential benefits of reducing the risk. This helps ensure that resources are allocated effectively.

Treating Risks

Risk treatment involves selecting and implementing appropriate controls to mitigate the identified risks. The goal is to reduce the likelihood and/or impact of risks to an acceptable level.

- **Risk Mitigation:** Implement controls to reduce the likelihood or impact of risks. In software development, this may include secure coding practices, code reviews, automated security testing, encryption, and access controls.
- **Risk Avoidance:** Modify the software development process to avoid certain risks entirely. For example, avoiding the use of third-party components with known vulnerabilities or not collecting certain types of sensitive data.
- **Risk Transfer:** Transfer the risk to a third party, such as through outsourcing or purchasing cyber insurance. This may be appropriate for risks that are difficult to manage internally.
- **Risk Acceptance:** Accept the risk if it falls within the organization's risk tolerance. This decision should be documented, along with the rationale for acceptance.
- **Implementing Controls:** Based on the selected risk treatment options, implement the necessary security controls. Ensure that these controls are integrated into the SDLC and that they are documented in the Statement of Applicability (SoA).

Monitoring and Reviewing Risks

Risk management is an ongoing process that requires continuous monitoring and review to ensure that the implemented controls remain effective and that new risks are identified and addressed.

- **Continuous Monitoring:** Monitor the effectiveness of security controls throughout the SDLC. This includes regular security testing, code audits, and vulnerability assessments.
- **Incident Tracking:** Track and analyze security incidents to determine if they are related to previously identified risks. Use this information to update the risk assessment and adjust controls as necessary.
- **Periodic Reviews:** Conduct regular reviews of the risk assessment process to ensure it remains aligned with the organization's objectives and the evolving threat landscape. This may involve reassessing risks in response to changes in technology, business processes, or regulatory requirements.
- **Feedback Loops:** Establish feedback loops that allow developers, security teams, and other stakeholders to report new risks or suggest improvements to the risk management process.

Documenting the Risk Assessment

Proper documentation is essential for ensuring transparency, accountability, and compliance with ISO 27001:2022. The risk assessment process and its outcomes should be thoroughly documented.

- **Risk Assessment Report:** Document the entire risk assessment process, including the context, identified risks, analysis results, risk ratings, and selected treatment options. This report serves as a key input for decision-making and audits.
- **Statement of Applicability (SoA):** The SoA should list all the controls selected to mitigate identified risks, along with justifications for their inclusion or exclusion. It should also reference relevant sections of the risk assessment report.
- **Risk Register:** Maintain a risk register that tracks all identified risks, their ratings, treatment decisions, and the status of implemented controls. The risk register should be regularly updated as part of the monitoring and review process.

Conclusion

A systematic methodology for risk assessment in software development is essential for identifying and mitigating risks that could compromise the security, integrity, and availability of software products. By following the steps outlined above—establishing the context, identifying risks, analyzing and evaluating them, treating the risks, and continuously monitoring and reviewing them—organizations can ensure that their software development processes are secure and aligned with ISO 27001:2022 standards. This proactive approach not only protects the organization's information assets but also enhances the overall quality and resilience of the software being developed.

Creating and Managing a Risk Treatment Plan

A Risk Treatment Plan (RTP) is a crucial element of an Information Security Management System (ISMS) under ISO 27001:2022. It outlines how identified risks will be addressed to reduce them to acceptable levels. The plan details the specific actions to be taken, the resources required, responsibilities, and timelines. Effective creation and management of an RTP ensures that information security risks are mitigated systematically and that the organization remains compliant with relevant standards and regulations.

Purpose of the Risk Treatment Plan

The primary purpose of the Risk Treatment Plan is to document the organization's approach to managing information security risks that have been identified during the risk assessment process. The RTP serves several key functions:

- **Mitigation of Risks:** The RTP provides a structured approach to reducing the likelihood and impact of identified risks.
- **Accountability:** The plan assigns responsibilities for implementing and monitoring risk treatment actions, ensuring that everyone involved knows their role.
- **Resource Allocation:** The RTP helps in planning and allocating the necessary resources, such as time, budget, and personnel, to address the risks.
- **Compliance:** The RTP ensures that the organization meets its legal, regulatory, and contractual obligations regarding risk management and information security.

Developing the Risk Treatment Plan

Creating an RTP involves several steps, starting from the selection of appropriate risk treatment options to the documentation and approval of the plan.

Step 1: Selecting Risk Treatment Options

For each identified risk, the organization must decide on the appropriate treatment strategy. ISO 27001:2022 provides four primary risk treatment options:

- **Risk Mitigation:** Implement controls to reduce the risk to an acceptable level. This is the most common approach and may involve technical controls (e.g., encryption, access controls), process changes (e.g., secure coding practices), or training (e.g., security awareness programs).
- **Risk Avoidance:** Alter the situation to avoid the risk altogether. For example, a company might choose not to develop a particular feature that poses high security risks or to avoid using certain third-party software components known to be vulnerable.
- **Risk Transfer:** Transfer the risk to a third party, such as by outsourcing certain activities or purchasing cyber insurance. This does not eliminate the risk but shifts its financial impact to another entity.
- **Risk Acceptance:** Accept the risk if it falls within the organization's risk tolerance. This decision should be based on a thorough analysis and documented justification.

Step 2: Defining Risk Treatment Actions

Once the treatment options are selected, specific actions need to be defined to implement these options. For each risk, the following should be documented:

- **Control Measures:** Identify the specific controls that will be implemented to mitigate the risk. These controls should be mapped to the relevant sections of ISO 27001:2022's Annex A, which provides a comprehensive list of control objectives and controls.
- **Responsibilities:** Assign responsibility for each action to specific individuals or teams. This ensures accountability and clarity regarding who is responsible for implementing each control.
- **Resources:** Identify the resources required to implement each control, including personnel, budget, and technology. This helps in planning and ensuring that the necessary support is available.
- **Timelines:** Establish a timeline for the implementation of each control, including start and end dates. Timelines help in tracking progress and ensuring that risk treatment actions are completed in a timely manner.

Step 3: Documenting the Risk Treatment Plan

The RTP should be documented in a clear and structured manner, making it easy to track and manage. The document should include:

- **Introduction:** A brief overview of the purpose and scope of the RTP.
- **Risk Identification:** A summary of the risks identified during the risk assessment process, including their likelihood, impact, and overall risk rating.
- **Treatment Actions:** Detailed descriptions of the treatment actions for each risk, including the selected treatment option, control measures, responsibilities, resources, and timelines.
- **Statement of Applicability (SoA):** A reference to the SoA, which lists all the controls selected for the ISMS, and justifications for their inclusion or exclusion. The RTP and SoA should be consistent with each other.
- **Approval:** A section for the formal approval of the RTP by top management or the ISMS steering committee. This ensures that the plan has the necessary endorsement and authority for implementation.

Step 4: Approval and Communication

Once the RTP is developed, it needs to be reviewed and approved by top management or the relevant governing body within the organization. Approval signifies that the organization is committed to implementing the plan and has allocated the necessary resources.

- **Top Management Review:** Ensure that top management reviews the RTP to verify that it aligns with the organization's risk appetite and business objectives.
- **Communication:** Communicate the RTP to all relevant stakeholders, including those responsible for implementing the controls, as well as any third parties involved in risk treatment actions. Clear communication ensures that everyone understands their roles and the importance of the actions to be taken.

Implementing the Risk Treatment Plan

Implementation of the RTP involves carrying out the actions defined in the plan. This phase requires careful coordination and monitoring to ensure that the controls are effectively implemented.

- **Action Execution:** Teams or individuals assigned to specific tasks should begin executing the risk treatment actions according to the timelines established in the RTP. This may involve deploying new technologies, updating processes, or conducting training sessions.
- **Resource Management:** Ensure that the required resources are available and properly utilized during implementation. Any resource constraints should be addressed promptly to avoid delays.

- **Collaboration and Coordination:** Effective implementation often requires collaboration across different departments, such as IT, legal, HR, and security. Regular coordination meetings and progress updates can help maintain momentum and address any issues that arise.

Monitoring and Reviewing the Risk Treatment Plan

Ongoing monitoring and review are critical to ensuring that the RTP remains effective and that the risk treatment actions achieve the desired outcomes.

- **Progress Tracking:** Regularly track the progress of risk treatment actions against the established timelines. This can be done through project management tools, status reports, and regular review meetings.
- **Effectiveness Evaluation:** Assess the effectiveness of the implemented controls in reducing the identified risks. This may involve conducting additional risk assessments, security audits, or performance testing.
- **Continuous Monitoring:** Implement continuous monitoring mechanisms to detect any changes in the risk environment that could impact the effectiveness of the controls. This includes monitoring for new vulnerabilities, changes in regulatory requirements, or shifts in business operations.
- **Periodic Reviews:** Conduct periodic reviews of the RTP to ensure it remains aligned with the organization's risk landscape and business objectives. Updates to the plan may be necessary if new risks emerge, if the effectiveness of controls changes, or if there are significant changes in the organization's operations or structure.

Updating and Improving the Risk Treatment Plan

The RTP should be a living document that evolves with the organization. Continuous improvement is essential to adapting to new challenges and ensuring ongoing protection against risks.

- **Lessons Learned:** After each risk treatment action is completed, conduct a lessons-learned review to identify what worked well and what could be improved. This feedback should be used to refine the RTP and the overall risk management process.
- **Updating Controls:** As new threats and vulnerabilities emerge, or as existing controls become obsolete, the RTP should be updated to reflect these changes. This may involve adding new controls, modifying existing ones, or retiring controls that are no longer effective.

- **Documentation Updates:** Ensure that all updates to the RTP are properly documented and communicated to relevant stakeholders. Maintain version control to track changes and ensure that everyone is working with the latest version of the plan.

Conclusion

Creating and managing a Risk Treatment Plan is a critical process in the effective management of information security risks within an organization. By systematically identifying, analyzing, treating, and monitoring risks, the RTP ensures that the organization can mitigate potential threats and maintain compliance with ISO 27001:2022 standards. A well-executed RTP not only protects the organization's information assets but also supports its overall business objectives by aligning risk management with strategic goals. Continuous review and improvement of the RTP are essential to maintaining its relevance and effectiveness in a dynamic risk environment.

Mitigating Risks Specific to Software Projects

Software projects inherently involve various risks that can impact the security, quality, and delivery of the final product. These risks arise from the complexities of software development, the evolving threat landscape, and the use of third-party components, among other factors. Effective risk mitigation strategies are essential to ensure that software projects meet their security, functional, and performance requirements while staying within budget and on schedule.

Understanding Software Project Risks

Before discussing mitigation strategies, it's essential to understand the types of risks typically associated with software projects:

- **Technical Risks:** These include risks related to software design, coding errors, integration challenges, and the use of new or unproven technologies.
- **Security Risks:** These risks pertain to vulnerabilities in the software that could be exploited by attackers, leading to data breaches, unauthorized access, or service disruptions.
- **Project Management Risks:** These include risks related to scope creep, timeline delays, inadequate resource allocation, and poor project management practices.
- **Operational Risks:** These involve risks related to the deployment, operation, and maintenance of the software, such as insufficient infrastructure or lack of monitoring.
- **Compliance Risks:** These are related to failing to meet regulatory, legal, or contractual obligations, which can result in fines, legal action, or reputational damage.

Mitigating Technical Risks

Technical risks are often the most challenging to manage in software projects due to the complexity and uncertainty involved. Effective mitigation strategies include:

- **Adopting Secure Coding Practices:**
  - **Code Reviews:** Implement regular code reviews to catch security flaws, coding errors, and deviations from coding standards. Peer

reviews and automated tools can help identify issues early in the development process.
    - **Static and Dynamic Analysis:** Use static and dynamic analysis tools to detect vulnerabilities in the codebase. These tools can identify common issues such as buffer overflows, SQL injection, and cross-site scripting (XSS).
    - **Secure Coding Standards:** Establish and enforce secure coding standards, such as those provided by OWASP or the SEI CERT, to minimize the introduction of vulnerabilities during development.
- **Conducting Rigorous Testing:**
    - **Unit Testing:** Ensure that all components are thoroughly unit tested to validate that they work as expected in isolation.
    - **Integration Testing:** Perform integration testing to identify issues that arise when individual components interact with each other.
    - **Penetration Testing:** Conduct regular penetration testing to simulate attacks on the software and identify vulnerabilities that could be exploited in a real-world scenario.
- **Managing Complexity:**
    - **Modular Design:** Use modular design principles to break down the software into manageable components, each with a well-defined interface. This reduces the complexity of the overall system and makes it easier to manage and test.
    - **Technical Debt Management:** Continuously monitor and manage technical debt, which refers to the trade-offs made during development that may lead to increased complexity and potential issues in the future. Addressing technical debt early can prevent it from becoming a significant risk later in the project.
- **Using Proven Technologies:**
    - **Technology Evaluation:** Before adopting new or unproven technologies, conduct thorough evaluations to assess their stability, security, and compatibility with existing systems.
    - **Pilot Projects:** Consider running pilot projects or proofs of concept (POCs) to test new technologies in a controlled environment before fully integrating them into the software project.

Mitigating Security Risks

Security risks are a significant concern in software projects, as vulnerabilities can lead to data breaches, financial losses, and reputational damage. Mitigation strategies include:

- **Implementing Security by Design:**

- **Threat Modeling:** Conduct threat modeling exercises early in the development process to identify potential security threats and design the software to mitigate these threats.
- **Security Requirements:** Clearly define security requirements alongside functional requirements to ensure that security is considered from the outset. These requirements should address access control, data protection, encryption, and logging.

- **Securing the Development Environment:**
  - **Access Control:** Implement strict access controls in the development environment to ensure that only authorized personnel can access the codebase and development tools.
  - **Environment Segmentation:** Segment development, testing, and production environments to reduce the risk of unauthorized access or accidental deployment of untested code.
  - **Continuous Monitoring:** Use continuous monitoring tools to detect suspicious activities, such as unauthorized code changes or access attempts, in the development environment.
- **Managing Third-Party Risks:**
  - **Third-Party Component Vetting:** Carefully vet third-party components, libraries, and APIs for security vulnerabilities before integrating them into the software. Use tools to track vulnerabilities in third-party software and ensure that components are regularly updated.
  - **Supplier Security Assessments:** Conduct security assessments of third-party suppliers to ensure they adhere to security best practices and contractual obligations.

Mitigating Project Management Risks

Effective project management is crucial to the success of software projects. Mitigation strategies for project management risks include:

- **Defining Clear Scope and Objectives:**
  - **Scope Definition:** Clearly define the project scope, including deliverables, timelines, and budget. Ensure that all stakeholders agree on the scope before the project begins to prevent scope creep.
  - **Change Management:** Implement a robust change management process to evaluate the impact of scope changes on the project timeline, budget, and resources. This helps prevent scope creep and ensures that changes are managed effectively.
- **Resource Management:**
  - **Resource Allocation:** Ensure that the project is adequately resourced with the necessary personnel, budget, and tools.

Regularly review resource allocation to address any gaps or shortages.
    - **Skill Development:** Invest in training and skill development for the project team to ensure they are equipped to handle the technical and security challenges of the project.
- **Risk Management:**
    - **Risk Register:** Maintain a risk register that tracks identified risks, their potential impact, and the mitigation strategies in place. Regularly review and update the risk register as the project progresses.
    - **Contingency Planning:** Develop contingency plans for high-impact risks, such as delays, budget overruns, or key personnel leaving the project. Contingency plans should outline the steps to be taken if these risks materialize.
- **Regular Monitoring and Reporting:**
    - **Progress Tracking:** Use project management tools to track progress against milestones and timelines. Regular status meetings and reports help ensure that the project stays on track.
    - **Stakeholder Communication:** Maintain open communication with stakeholders, providing regular updates on project status, risks, and issues. This helps manage expectations and ensures that stakeholders are informed of any changes.

Mitigating Operational Risks

Operational risks can affect the deployment, maintenance, and operation of the software. Mitigation strategies include:

- **Infrastructure Readiness:**
    - **Infrastructure Assessment:** Assess the readiness of the infrastructure to support the software, including server capacity, network bandwidth, and redundancy. Ensure that the infrastructure is scalable and resilient.
    - **Disaster Recovery Planning:** Develop and test disaster recovery plans to ensure that the software can be quickly restored in the event of a failure or security incident.
- **Deployment and Release Management:**
    - **Automated Deployment:** Use automated deployment tools to reduce the risk of human error during the release process. Automation helps ensure consistency and repeatability in deployments.

- **Rollback Procedures:** Establish rollback procedures that allow for quick reversion to a previous stable version of the software if issues are encountered during deployment.

- **Post-Deployment Monitoring:**
  - **Performance Monitoring:** Implement performance monitoring tools to track the software's performance in the production environment. This helps identify and address issues before they impact users.
  - **Security Monitoring:** Use security monitoring tools to detect and respond to security incidents in real-time. Regularly review logs and alerts to ensure ongoing security.

Mitigating Compliance Risks

Compliance risks involve failing to meet legal, regulatory, or contractual obligations. Mitigation strategies include:

- **Regulatory Compliance:**
  - **Regulatory Requirements:** Identify all relevant regulatory requirements, such as GDPR, HIPAA, or PCI DSS, that apply to the software project. Ensure that these requirements are incorporated into the project's security and privacy controls.
  - **Data Protection:** Implement data protection measures, such as encryption, data masking, and access controls, to ensure compliance with data protection regulations.
- **Contractual Compliance:**
  - **Contract Review:** Review contracts with customers, suppliers, and partners to identify any security or compliance obligations. Ensure that these obligations are addressed in the software development process.
  - **Third-Party Audits:** Conduct regular audits of third-party vendors to ensure they comply with contractual security requirements.
- **Documentation and Reporting:**
  - **Compliance Documentation:** Maintain comprehensive documentation of compliance-related activities, including risk assessments, security controls, and audit reports. This documentation is essential for demonstrating compliance during audits or inspections.
  - **Audit Preparation:** Prepare for audits by conducting internal reviews and ensuring that all compliance-related documentation is up to date and readily accessible.

Conclusion

Mitigating risks specific to software projects requires a comprehensive approach that addresses technical, security, project management, operational, and compliance risks. By implementing the strategies outlined above, organizations can reduce the likelihood and impact of these risks, ensuring that software projects are completed successfully, securely, and in compliance with relevant standards and regulations. Effective risk mitigation not only protects the organization's information assets but also contributes to the overall quality, reliability, and success of the software product.

Chapter 5

Information Security Objectives

Setting SMART Security Goals

Setting effective security goals is a crucial step in managing an organization's information security. These goals guide the development and implementation of security strategies and help ensure that the organization's Information Security Management System (ISMS) is aligned with its business objectives. The SMART criteria—Specific, Measurable, Achievable, Relevant, and Time-bound—provide a framework for setting clear and actionable security goals.

What Are SMART Security Goals?

SMART security goals are designed to provide clarity and direction by defining specific targets that the organization aims to achieve within its security program. Each component of the SMART acronym serves a purpose in ensuring that the goals are realistic, actionable, and aligned with the organization's broader objectives.

- **Specific:** Goals should be clear and unambiguous, detailing exactly what is to be achieved.
- **Measurable:** Goals should include criteria to track progress and determine when the goal has been met.
- **Achievable:** Goals should be realistic and attainable, considering the organization's resources and constraints.
- **Relevant:** Goals should align with the organization's broader business objectives and address its key risks and security priorities.
- **Time-bound:** Goals should have a defined timeline for completion, ensuring a sense of urgency and focus.

Setting Specific Security Goals

Specificity in goal-setting ensures that everyone involved understands exactly what is expected. This clarity helps prevent misunderstandings and ensures that efforts are focused on achieving the defined objectives.

- **Example:** Instead of setting a vague goal like "Improve network security," a specific goal would be "Implement multi-factor authentication (MFA) for all remote access by employees."
- **Best Practices:**
  - Clearly define what you want to accomplish.

    - Include details such as who is responsible, what resources are needed, and which systems or processes are involved.
    - Avoid broad or generalized statements.

Setting Measurable Security Goals

Measurability allows the organization to track progress toward the goal and determine when it has been achieved. This involves defining clear metrics or key performance indicators (KPIs) that can be used to assess progress.

- **Example:** "Reduce the number of critical vulnerabilities in production systems by 50% within six months."
- **Best Practices:**
    - Define specific metrics to measure progress (e.g., the number of vulnerabilities, the percentage of systems with updated patches).
    - Use tools and processes that can reliably track and report on these metrics.
    - Set benchmarks or targets that indicate when the goal is met.

Setting Achievable Security Goals

Goals must be realistic and achievable given the organization's current resources, capabilities, and constraints. Setting unattainable goals can lead to frustration and disengagement.

- **Example:** "Conduct phishing awareness training for 100% of employees within the next quarter" is achievable if the organization has the necessary training resources and time.
- **Best Practices:**
    - Assess the organization's current capabilities, resources, and constraints before setting goals.
    - Ensure that the goals are challenging yet attainable with the available resources.
    - Consider potential barriers and plan for how to overcome them.

Setting Relevant Security Goals

Relevance ensures that the goals are aligned with the organization's broader objectives and address its most pressing security risks. Relevant goals contribute to the overall effectiveness of the ISMS and support the organization's strategic priorities.

- **Example:** "Achieve ISO 27001:2022 certification within 12 months to enhance customer trust and meet contractual obligations."
- **Best Practices:**

    - Align security goals with the organization’s business strategy, mission, and risk profile.
    - Prioritize goals that address critical risks or regulatory requirements.
    - Ensure that goals contribute to the organization’s long-term security and operational effectiveness.

Setting Time-bound Security Goals

Time-bound goals have a clear deadline or timeframe for completion. This adds a sense of urgency and helps ensure that the organization remains focused on achieving the goal within the specified period.

- **Example:** "Complete the migration of all critical applications to a secure cloud environment within nine months."
- **Best Practices:**
    - Set a realistic deadline for achieving the goal.
    - Consider the time required for planning, implementation, testing, and validation.
    - Break down longer-term goals into smaller, time-bound milestones to track progress.

Examples of SMART Security Goals

Here are some examples of SMART security goals that an organization might set as part of its ISMS:

- **Specific:** "Implement encryption for all sensitive customer data stored in databases by the end of Q2."
- **Measurable:** "Reduce the average time to respond to security incidents from 8 hours to 4 hours within the next six months."
- **Achievable:** "Train 95% of employees on the organization’s information security policies within three months using the existing e-learning platform."
- **Relevant:** "Develop and implement a secure DevOps pipeline within the next year to support the rapid and secure deployment of software updates."
- **Time-bound:** "Complete a full internal audit of the ISMS by the end of the fiscal year to prepare for the upcoming ISO 27001:2022 certification audit."

Monitoring and Reviewing SMART Security Goals

Setting SMART security goals is just the beginning. Regular monitoring and review are essential to ensure that the organization stays on track and makes necessary adjustments along the way.

- **Tracking Progress:** Use dashboards, reports, and meetings to track progress against each goal. Ensure that responsible parties provide regular updates.
- **Adjusting Goals:** If circumstances change—such as new threats emerging or resources becoming limited—be prepared to adjust the goals accordingly.
- **Reviewing Outcomes:** After a goal is achieved, review the process to identify lessons learned and areas for improvement. This helps refine future goal-setting and enhances the effectiveness of the ISMS.

Conclusion

Setting SMART security goals is a powerful way to ensure that an organization's information security efforts are focused, measurable, and aligned with its overall business strategy. By defining Specific, Measurable, Achievable, Relevant, and Time-bound goals, organizations can create a clear roadmap for enhancing their security posture and achieving meaningful results. Regular monitoring and review of these goals help ensure continuous improvement and long-term success in managing information security.

Aligning Security Objectives with Business Outcomes

Aligning security objectives with business outcomes is critical to ensuring that an organization's Information Security Management System (ISMS) supports its overall strategic goals. When security initiatives are closely tied to business outcomes, they not only protect the organization's information assets but also contribute to achieving broader business objectives such as growth, innovation, customer trust, and regulatory compliance. This alignment ensures that security is seen as a business enabler rather than a cost center.

Understanding Business Outcomes

Before aligning security objectives with business outcomes, it's essential to clearly understand what the organization aims to achieve. Common business outcomes include:

- **Revenue Growth:** Expanding market share, increasing sales, and entering new markets.
- **Customer Trust and Satisfaction:** Building and maintaining trust with customers through reliable and secure services.
- **Operational Efficiency:** Streamlining processes, reducing costs, and improving productivity.
- **Regulatory Compliance:** Meeting legal, regulatory, and industry standards to avoid fines and legal actions.
- **Innovation:** Developing new products, services, or business models to stay competitive.
- **Risk Management:** Identifying, assessing, and mitigating risks that could impact the business.

Identifying Relevant Security Objectives

Security objectives should be designed to support and enhance these business outcomes. The following are examples of security objectives that align with common business outcomes:

- **For Revenue Growth:** Implement robust security measures to protect intellectual property and customer data, enabling the organization to confidently expand into new markets or launch new products.

- **For Customer Trust and Satisfaction:** Enhance data protection and privacy practices to build customer trust, leading to increased customer retention and positive brand reputation.
- **For Operational Efficiency:** Automate security processes, such as threat detection and incident response, to reduce the time and cost associated with managing security incidents.
- **For Regulatory Compliance:** Ensure continuous compliance with relevant regulations and standards, such as GDPR, HIPAA, or PCI DSS, to avoid penalties and maintain the organization's ability to operate in regulated markets.
- **For Innovation:** Integrate security into the product development lifecycle (DevSecOps) to enable the rapid and secure development of new products and services.
- **For Risk Management:** Develop a comprehensive risk management framework that identifies, assesses, and mitigates risks, ensuring that the organization can operate smoothly without major disruptions.

Setting SMART Security Objectives

To effectively align security objectives with business outcomes, it's important to set SMART (Specific, Measurable, Achievable, Relevant, and Time-bound) security goals. These goals should directly contribute to achieving the desired business outcomes.

- **Specific:** Clearly define what the security objective aims to achieve and how it supports a specific business outcome.

  Example: "Implement encryption for all customer data to enhance customer trust and comply with GDPR."
- **Measurable:** Establish metrics to track progress and success, ensuring that the security objective is quantifiable.

  Example: "Achieve a 90% reduction in security incidents affecting customer data within 12 months."
- **Achievable:** Ensure that the security objective is realistic given the organization's resources and capabilities.

  Example: "Deploy multi-factor authentication (MFA) for all employees within the next quarter to secure access to critical systems."
- **Relevant:** Align the security objective with key business outcomes to ensure it adds value to the organization.

  Example: "Develop a secure DevOps pipeline to accelerate the release of new features, supporting the organization's innovation strategy."

- **Time-bound:** Set a clear timeline for achieving the security objective to maintain focus and urgency.

  Example: "Complete ISO 27001:2022 certification within 18 months to enhance market credibility and meet contractual obligations."

Mapping Security Objectives to Business Outcomes

To ensure alignment, map each security objective to one or more business outcomes. This mapping helps illustrate how security initiatives contribute to the organization's strategic goals and makes it easier to communicate the value of security to stakeholders.

Example Mapping:

- **Security Objective:** Implement a comprehensive incident response plan.
- **Mapped Business Outcome:** Enhance operational efficiency by reducing downtime and minimizing the impact of security incidents on business operations.
- **Security Objective:** Achieve ISO 27001:2022 certification.
- **Mapped Business Outcome:** Increase customer trust and satisfaction by demonstrating a commitment to high standards of information security.
- **Security Objective:** Deploy a secure DevOps pipeline.
- **Mapped Business Outcome:** Support innovation by enabling the rapid and secure development of new products and features.

Engaging Stakeholders in the Alignment Process

Effective alignment requires the involvement of both security and business stakeholders. Engaging these stakeholders ensures that security objectives are understood, supported, and integrated into broader business strategies.

- **Collaborate with Business Leaders:** Work closely with business leaders to understand their strategic goals and priorities. This collaboration helps ensure that security objectives are aligned with what the business is trying to achieve.
- **Communicate the Value of Security:** Clearly articulate how security objectives contribute to business outcomes. Use metrics and case studies to demonstrate the impact of security initiatives on revenue, customer trust, compliance, and risk management.
- **Establish Cross-Functional Teams:** Create cross-functional teams that include representatives from security, IT, operations, and business units. These teams can work together to ensure that security is integrated into all business processes and decision-making.

Measuring and Reporting on Security Objectives

To ensure ongoing alignment, it's important to regularly measure and report on the progress of security objectives. This involves:

- **Tracking Metrics:** Use defined metrics to monitor the progress of security objectives. For example, track the number of security incidents, the time taken to detect and respond to threats, or the percentage of systems compliant with security standards.
- **Regular Reporting:** Provide regular updates to business leaders and other stakeholders on the status of security objectives and their impact on business outcomes. Use dashboards, reports, and presentations to communicate results effectively.
- **Adjusting Objectives:** Be prepared to adjust security objectives as business needs evolve. Regularly review and refine security goals to ensure they remain aligned with the organization's changing priorities and the evolving threat landscape.

Continuous Improvement and Adaptation

The alignment of security objectives with business outcomes should be an ongoing process. As the business environment changes, so too should the security strategy. Continuous improvement involves:

- **Feedback Loops:** Establish feedback loops between security teams and business units to ensure that security objectives are meeting business needs. Use this feedback to make adjustments and improvements.
- **Adaptive Strategy:** Be agile in responding to changes in the business environment, such as new market opportunities, emerging technologies, or shifts in customer expectations. Update security objectives as needed to support these changes.
- **Learning from Incidents:** Use lessons learned from security incidents or near-misses to refine security objectives and improve alignment with business outcomes.

Conclusion

Aligning security objectives with business outcomes is essential for ensuring that security initiatives support the organization's strategic goals and add tangible value. By setting SMART security goals, mapping them to business outcomes, engaging stakeholders, and continuously measuring and improving performance, organizations can create a security program that not only protects information assets but also drives business success.

This alignment transforms security from a purely protective function into a strategic enabler of growth, innovation, and customer trust.

Continuous Improvement Through Regular Review

Continuous improvement is a fundamental principle of effective information security management, particularly within the framework of ISO 27001:2022. Regular review processes ensure that an organization's Information Security Management System (ISMS) remains effective, adapts to evolving threats, and continues to align with business objectives. By incorporating regular assessments, audits, feedback loops, and updates, organizations can drive continuous improvement in their security practices, making them more resilient, agile, and capable of addressing emerging challenges.

Importance of Continuous Improvement

Continuous improvement in information security involves making iterative enhancements to the ISMS based on the results of regular reviews, audits, incident responses, and changes in the organization's risk landscape. The key benefits include:

- **Adaptability to New Threats:** Regular reviews help organizations adapt to emerging security threats and vulnerabilities by proactively updating controls and strategies.
- **Enhanced Security Posture:** By continuously refining security measures, organizations can maintain a strong defense against both internal and external threats.
- **Compliance Maintenance:** Regular reviews ensure that the organization stays compliant with evolving legal, regulatory, and contractual obligations.
- **Operational Efficiency:** Improving processes and security controls can enhance the organization's operational efficiency and reduce the impact of security incidents.

Types of Regular Reviews

There are several types of reviews that contribute to continuous improvement, each with a specific focus:

Internal Audits

Internal audits are conducted periodically to assess the effectiveness of the ISMS, ensure compliance with policies and standards, and identify areas for improvement.

- **Scope:** Internal audits cover a wide range of topics, from the effectiveness of security controls to the organization's adherence to ISO 27001:2022 requirements.
- **Frequency:** Internal audits should be conducted at least annually, but more frequent audits may be necessary for high-risk areas.
- **Outcomes:** The results of internal audits should lead to corrective actions, improvements to controls, and adjustments to policies where necessary.

Management Reviews

Management reviews are high-level assessments conducted by top management to evaluate the overall performance of the ISMS and its alignment with business objectives.

- **Scope:** These reviews assess the adequacy of resources, the effectiveness of security policies, the outcomes of audits, and the alignment of the ISMS with strategic goals.
- **Frequency:** Management reviews should be conducted annually or more frequently if significant changes occur within the organization or its risk environment.
- **Outcomes:** The findings from management reviews should drive updates to the ISMS, including changes to security objectives, policies, and resource allocations.

Risk Assessments

Regular risk assessments are essential to identify new risks and reassess existing ones based on changes in the organization's operations, technology, and threat landscape.

- **Scope:** Risk assessments evaluate threats, vulnerabilities, and the potential impact of risks on the organization's information assets.
- **Frequency:** Risk assessments should be conducted annually, as well as when significant changes occur (e.g., the introduction of new technology, changes in business processes, or major security incidents).
- **Outcomes:** The results of risk assessments inform updates to the risk treatment plan, including the introduction of new controls or the modification of existing ones.

Security Incident Reviews

After security incidents, post-incident reviews (also known as post-mortem analyses) are conducted to identify the root cause of the incident, assess the effectiveness of the response, and determine what improvements can be made to prevent future occurrences.

- **Scope:** Incident reviews focus on identifying weaknesses in the ISMS that allowed the incident to occur and evaluating the response process.
- **Frequency:** Incident reviews are conducted after every significant security incident.
- **Outcomes:** These reviews lead to corrective actions, such as improving incident response procedures, strengthening controls, or addressing gaps in employee training.

Compliance Reviews

Compliance reviews ensure that the organization adheres to legal, regulatory, and contractual requirements, particularly in sectors with stringent data protection or security standards.

- **Scope:** These reviews assess the organization's compliance with regulations such as GDPR, HIPAA, or industry standards like PCI DSS.
- **Frequency:** Compliance reviews should be conducted annually or whenever regulatory requirements change.
- **Outcomes:** The results of compliance reviews should lead to updates in policies, procedures, and security controls to maintain compliance.

The Continuous Improvement Process

Continuous improvement follows a structured process that integrates feedback from regular reviews and assessments into the ongoing development of the ISMS. This process is typically based on the **Plan-Do-Check-Act (PDCA)** cycle:

Plan: Establish Objectives and Processes

- **Objective Setting:** Based on the outcomes of regular reviews, establish clear objectives for improving the ISMS. Objectives may include reducing the number of security incidents, enhancing incident response times, or achieving certification for a new standard.
- **Action Plans:** Develop detailed action plans to achieve these objectives. This may involve implementing new controls, refining existing processes, or conducting additional training for staff.

Do: Implement the Improvements

- **Execution:** Implement the improvements defined in the action plan. This could involve deploying new security technologies, updating policies, or enhancing monitoring and detection capabilities.
- **Training and Awareness:** Ensure that employees are trained on new processes and controls. Regular security awareness training helps foster a culture of continuous improvement.

Check: Monitor and Measure Effectiveness

- **Performance Measurement:** Use metrics and KPIs to monitor the effectiveness of the improvements. For example, track the number of security incidents, the time taken to detect and respond to threats, or the success rate of security audits.
- **Audit and Review:** Conduct follow-up audits and reviews to assess whether the implemented changes are delivering the desired outcomes.

Act: Make Adjustments and Further Improvements

- **Feedback and Refinement:** Based on the results of the monitoring and review phases, make further adjustments to the ISMS. This might involve refining controls, modifying processes, or addressing newly identified risks.
- **Cycle Continuation:** Repeat the PDCA cycle regularly to ensure continuous improvement. Each iteration of the cycle should build on the previous one, driving incremental enhancements to the ISMS.

Key Areas for Continuous Improvement

Certain areas of the ISMS require ongoing focus to ensure they remain effective and aligned with business objectives:

- **Security Policies and Procedures:** Regularly update policies and procedures to reflect new threats, changes in technology, and evolving regulatory requirements.
- **Technology and Tools:** Continuously evaluate and adopt new security technologies and tools that can improve the organization's ability to detect, prevent, and respond to threats.
- **Employee Training and Awareness:** Regularly refresh and update security training to ensure that employees are aware of current threats and understand their roles in protecting information assets.
- **Incident Response:** Continuously refine incident response plans to improve detection, containment, and recovery times. Lessons learned from past incidents should inform these improvements.

Creating a Culture of Continuous Improvement

For continuous improvement to be successful, it must become part of the organization's culture. This involves:

- **Leadership Commitment:** Ensure that top management is committed to continuous improvement by actively participating in reviews, allocating resources, and promoting a culture of learning and adaptation.
- **Employee Engagement:** Engage employees at all levels in the continuous improvement process. Encourage them to provide feedback on security processes, report incidents, and suggest improvements.
- **Reward and Recognition:** Recognize and reward individuals or teams who contribute to the continuous improvement of the ISMS. This helps reinforce the importance of security and motivates others to participate.

Monitoring and Reporting on Continuous Improvement

Regular reporting on the progress of continuous improvement efforts is essential for maintaining momentum and ensuring accountability. Key activities include:

- **Progress Reports:** Provide regular updates to top management and key stakeholders on the progress of improvement initiatives, including metrics on performance and the status of action plans.
- **Dashboard Monitoring:** Use dashboards and other reporting tools to provide real-time visibility into the effectiveness of security controls and the progress of continuous improvement efforts.
- **Management Reviews:** Conduct formal management reviews at least annually to assess the overall effectiveness of the ISMS and its alignment with business objectives.

Conclusion

Continuous improvement through regular review is essential for maintaining an effective ISMS that can adapt to new threats, changing business environments, and evolving compliance requirements. By conducting regular audits, reviews, and assessments, and by following the Plan-Do-Check-Act cycle, organizations can ensure that their security practices are not only reactive but proactive, continuously enhancing their security posture and resilience. This ongoing commitment to improvement helps protect information assets, support business objectives, and build a strong culture of security throughout the organization.

Part 4

Operational Excellence

Chapter 6

Integrating ISMS into the SDLC

Best Practices for Embedding Security into Every Phase of the SDLC

Integrating security into every phase of the Software Development Lifecycle (SDLC) is essential to building secure software products. By embedding security practices from the initial planning stages through to deployment and maintenance, organizations can mitigate risks, prevent vulnerabilities, and ensure that security is an integral part of the development process rather than an afterthought. Here are the best practices for embedding security into each phase of the SDLC:

Planning and Requirements Gathering

Security should be considered from the very beginning of a software project, during the planning and requirements gathering phase.

- **Security Requirements Identification:**
  - **Define Security Requirements:** Clearly define security requirements alongside functional requirements. These should include data protection, access control, authentication, and compliance with relevant regulations (e.g., GDPR, HIPAA).
  - **Involve Security Experts:** Involve security experts early in the project to identify potential security risks and requirements. Their input helps ensure that security considerations are fully integrated into the project scope.
  - **Risk Assessment:** Conduct a preliminary risk assessment to identify potential security threats and vulnerabilities. This assessment will inform the security requirements and guide the design phase.
- **Threat Modeling:**
  - **Conduct Threat Modeling:** Identify potential threats to the system, such as unauthorized access, data breaches, or denial of service attacks. Use threat modeling techniques like STRIDE (Spoofing, Tampering, Repudiation, Information Disclosure, Denial of Service, Elevation of Privilege) to systematically assess risks.
  - **Prioritize Risks:** Prioritize identified risks based on their potential impact and likelihood, and incorporate mitigation strategies into the project plan.

Design

The design phase is critical for incorporating security into the software architecture and overall system design.

- **Secure Architecture Design:**
  - **Adopt Secure Design Principles:** Incorporate secure design principles such as least privilege, defense in depth, and fail-safe defaults into the software architecture. These principles help create a robust and resilient system.
  - **Data Flow Diagrams (DFDs):** Use DFDs to map out how data moves through the system, identifying where security controls should be implemented (e.g., encryption, access controls).
- **Design Reviews:**
  - **Conduct Security Design Reviews:** Hold design review meetings that include security experts to assess the proposed architecture and design. Identify and address potential security weaknesses before development begins.
  - **Use Security Checklists:** Utilize security checklists specific to the design phase to ensure that all security aspects are considered, such as secure coding practices, data encryption, and authentication mechanisms.
- **Integration of Security Tools:**
  - **Plan for Security Tools Integration:** Plan for the integration of security tools, such as static analysis tools, in the development process. Ensure that these tools are aligned with the chosen development framework and environment.

Development

During the development phase, secure coding practices and continuous security testing are essential to prevent the introduction of vulnerabilities.

- **Secure Coding Practices:**
  - **Follow Secure Coding Standards:** Adhere to established secure coding standards, such as those provided by OWASP or the CERT Secure Coding Guidelines. These standards help developers avoid common vulnerabilities like SQL injection, cross-site scripting (XSS), and buffer overflows.
  - **Code Reviews:** Implement peer code reviews with a focus on security. Ensure that experienced developers and security experts review the code to identify and remediate security issues early.

- **Use of Security Tools:**
  - **Static Application Security Testing (SAST):** Integrate SAST tools into the development environment to automatically analyze code for security vulnerabilities as it is written. This allows for early detection and resolution of issues.
  - **Dependency Scanning:** Use tools to scan third-party libraries and dependencies for known vulnerabilities. Regularly update these components to ensure they remain secure.
- **Secure Configuration Management:**
  - **Version Control:** Implement strict version control policies to ensure that only authorized changes are made to the codebase. Use tools like Git to track changes and enforce secure development practices.
  - **Secure Build Environment:** Ensure that the build environment is secure, with restricted access and monitoring to prevent unauthorized modifications to the code.

Testing

Security testing is a vital part of the SDLC, ensuring that the software meets its security requirements and is free from vulnerabilities.

- **Security Testing Integration:**
  - **Dynamic Application Security Testing (DAST):** Implement DAST tools to test the application in a runtime environment. These tools simulate attacks and identify vulnerabilities such as insecure configurations, injection flaws, and security misconfigurations.
  - **Interactive Application Security Testing (IAST):** Use IAST tools that combine elements of both SAST and DAST, providing real-time feedback on security vulnerabilities during testing.
- **Penetration Testing:**
  - **Conduct Penetration Tests:** Perform penetration testing on the software to identify vulnerabilities that could be exploited by attackers. Penetration tests should simulate real-world attack scenarios to assess the effectiveness of security controls.
  - **Test Security Controls:** Validate that all implemented security controls, such as encryption, access controls, and input validation, function as intended and are resistant to bypass techniques.
- **Automated and Manual Testing:**
  - **Automated Security Testing:** Automate security testing as much as possible to ensure consistent and repeatable results. However, complement automation with manual testing for areas where

human insight is critical, such as logic flaws or complex security scenarios.
    - **Continuous Testing:** Integrate security testing into the Continuous Integration/Continuous Deployment (CI/CD) pipeline to ensure that every build is tested for security vulnerabilities before deployment.

Deployment

Security considerations should extend into the deployment phase, ensuring that the software is securely deployed and configured in its production environment.

- **Secure Deployment Practices:**
    - **Automated Deployment:** Use automated deployment tools to minimize human error and ensure that security configurations are consistently applied across environments.
    - **Configuration Management:** Implement secure configuration management practices, such as using configuration scripts or templates that enforce secure settings. Avoid using default credentials or configurations that could be exploited.
- **Environment Hardening:**
    - **Harden Servers and Environments:** Ensure that servers and environments where the software will be deployed are hardened. This includes disabling unnecessary services, applying security patches, and configuring firewalls.
    - **Secure Data Transfers:** Use secure protocols (e.g., HTTPS, SFTP) to protect data during transfer between environments. Ensure that sensitive data is encrypted at rest and in transit.
- **Access Control and Monitoring:**
    - **Access Controls:** Implement strict access controls for production environments, ensuring that only authorized personnel have access to deploy or modify the software.
    - **Security Monitoring:** Set up monitoring tools to continuously monitor the deployed software for suspicious activities or security breaches. This includes logging and alerting on critical security events.

Maintenance and Operations

After deployment, ongoing maintenance and monitoring are necessary to ensure the software remains secure throughout its lifecycle.

- **Patch Management:**
  - **Regular Updates:** Implement a patch management process to regularly update the software, third-party libraries, and underlying infrastructure with security patches. Address vulnerabilities promptly to minimize exposure.
  - **Vulnerability Management:** Continuously scan for new vulnerabilities in the software and its dependencies. Establish a process for evaluating and prioritizing the remediation of vulnerabilities based on their risk.
- **Security Monitoring and Incident Response:**
  - **Continuous Monitoring:** Use security monitoring tools (e.g., SIEM) to detect and respond to security incidents in real-time. Monitor logs, network traffic, and user activities for signs of compromise.
  - **Incident Response Plan:** Develop and maintain an incident response plan to quickly and effectively respond to security incidents. Conduct regular drills and tabletop exercises to ensure that the response team is prepared.
- **Regular Security Audits:**
  - **Conduct Security Audits:** Perform regular security audits of the software and its environment to identify and address any emerging risks. Audits should include both internal assessments and external penetration testing.
  - **Compliance Monitoring:** Ensure that the software remains compliant with relevant regulations and standards throughout its lifecycle. Regularly review and update security policies and procedures to reflect changes in the regulatory landscape.

Decommissioning

When software reaches the end of its lifecycle, decommissioning must be handled securely to prevent data leaks or unauthorized access.

- **Data Sanitization:**
  - **Secure Data Deletion:** Ensure that all data associated with the software is securely deleted or sanitized according to best practices. Use data wiping tools that comply with industry standards (e.g., NIST, DoD) for data destruction.
  - **Backup Management:** Review and securely delete or archive any backups of the software or its data, ensuring that no sensitive information is left accessible.

- **Retirement of Access Credentials:**
  - **Revoke Access:** Revoke all access credentials, including user accounts and API keys, associated with the software. Ensure that these credentials cannot be used to access other systems.
  - **Decommissioning Documentation:** Document the decommissioning process, including the steps taken to securely retire the software and its associated data. Maintain records for compliance and auditing purposes.

Conclusion

Embedding security into every phase of the SDLC is essential for developing robust, secure software that can withstand the evolving threat landscape. By adopting the best practices outlined above, organizations can ensure that security is not an afterthought but a fundamental aspect of the software development process. This proactive approach not only helps prevent vulnerabilities but also enhances the overall quality, reliability, and compliance of the software, ultimately protecting the organization and its customers from potential security breaches.

Threat Modeling and Secure Design Principles

Threat modeling and secure design principles are foundational practices in building secure software. They help identify potential threats early in the software development lifecycle (SDLC) and guide the design of systems that are resilient against these threats. By systematically analyzing potential risks and applying best practices in secure design, organizations can reduce vulnerabilities and enhance the security posture of their applications.

Understanding Threat Modeling

Threat modeling is a structured approach used to identify, assess, and address potential security threats to a system. It involves thinking like an attacker to understand how they might exploit vulnerabilities in the system. The primary goal of threat modeling is to identify and mitigate security risks during the design and development phases, reducing the likelihood of security issues later in the SDLC.

Key Steps in Threat Modeling

Define the Scope:

- **Identify Assets:** Determine what needs protection, such as sensitive data, critical system components, or intellectual property.
- **Determine Boundaries:** Identify the scope of the threat modeling exercise, including the systems, applications, and data that will be analyzed.

Create an Architecture Overview:

- **Diagram the System:** Use data flow diagrams (DFDs) to visually represent the system's architecture, including components, data flows, and external entities.
- **Identify Entry Points:** Highlight all the points where an attacker could potentially interact with the system, such as APIs, user interfaces, or network interfaces.

Identify Threats:

- **Use Threat Libraries:** Leverage threat libraries like STRIDE (Spoofing, Tampering, Repudiation, Information Disclosure, Denial of Service, Elevation of Privilege) to systematically identify potential threats to the system.
- **Think Like an Attacker:** Consider how an attacker might exploit vulnerabilities at each entry point or weak link in the system.

Analyze Threats:

- **Assess Risk:** Evaluate the likelihood and impact of each identified threat. Consider factors such as the sophistication of potential attackers, the value of the assets, and the effectiveness of existing controls.
- **Prioritize Threats:** Rank the threats based on their potential impact and the feasibility of mitigation. Focus on high-risk threats that could have significant consequences.

Define Mitigation Strategies:

- **Develop Countermeasures:** Propose and implement security controls to mitigate identified threats. These might include encryption, access controls, input validation, or logging.
- **Integrate with Design:** Ensure that the proposed mitigations are integrated into the system's design and development processes.

Validate and Iterate:

- **Review and Test:** Continuously validate the effectiveness of the threat mitigations through testing, such as security reviews, penetration testing, or red teaming.
- **Iterate the Model:** Update the threat model as the system evolves, incorporating changes in architecture, new features, or emerging threats.

Common Threat Modeling Frameworks

- **STRIDE:** A widely used framework that categorizes threats into six types: Spoofing identity, Tampering with data, Repudiation, Information disclosure, Denial of service, and Elevation of privilege.
- **DREAD:** A risk assessment model that rates threats based on five criteria: Damage potential, Reproducibility, Exploitability, Affected users, and Discoverability.

- **PASTA (Process for Attack Simulation and Threat Analysis):** A seven-step risk-centric methodology that focuses on simulating attacks and analyzing the impact on business objectives.
- **MITRE ATT&CK:** A knowledge base of adversary tactics and techniques, which can be used to identify and categorize potential threats during threat modeling.

Secure Design Principles

Secure design principles are guidelines that help create software systems that are resistant to attacks and resilient in the face of security incidents. These principles should be applied throughout the design and development phases to ensure that security is an integral part of the software architecture.

Key Secure Design Principles

- **Least Privilege:**
  - **Minimize Access:** Ensure that users and systems have the minimum level of access necessary to perform their functions. This reduces the potential damage that could result from a compromised account or system.
  - **Use Role-Based Access Control (RBAC):** Implement RBAC to enforce least privilege by assigning permissions based on roles rather than individual users.
- **Defense in Depth:**
  - **Layered Security:** Implement multiple layers of security controls throughout the system. This ensures that if one layer is compromised, others remain in place to protect the system.
  - **Redundancy:** Use redundant controls, such as combining firewalls with intrusion detection systems, to provide multiple levels of protection.
- **Fail-Safe Defaults:**
  - **Default to Secure:** Configure systems and applications to default to secure settings. For example, deny access by default and explicitly grant access where necessary.
  - **Error Handling:** Ensure that error handling does not expose sensitive information or inadvertently weaken security. Errors should be logged securely and should not reveal details to attackers.

- **Separation of Duties:**
  - **Distribute Responsibilities:** Ensure that critical tasks are divided among multiple users or systems to reduce the risk of fraud or error. For example, separate the roles of developer, tester, and deployer.
  - **Access Segregation:** Segregate access to different parts of the system based on user roles and responsibilities to minimize the impact of a compromised account.
- **Minimize Attack Surface:**
  - **Reduce Complexity:** Simplify the system architecture to reduce the number of potential entry points for attackers. Remove unnecessary features, services, and code that could introduce vulnerabilities.
  - **Patch Management:** Regularly update and patch software components, libraries, and systems to reduce exposure to known vulnerabilities.
- **Secure Defaults:**
  - **Default Secure Settings:** Configure systems with security best practices out of the box. Users should not have to take additional steps to secure the system.
  - **Documented Security Configurations:** Provide clear documentation for secure configurations to ensure that users can maintain a secure posture after deployment.
- **Complete Mediation:**
  - **Always Validate Requests:** Ensure that every access request is validated and authenticated, even if it comes from a trusted source. This prevents unauthorized access through bypassing controls.
  - **Consistent Enforcement:** Apply security checks consistently across all components and interfaces of the system to avoid weak points.
- **Security by Design:**
  - **Build Security In:** Integrate security considerations into every phase of the SDLC, from planning through to deployment. Security should not be bolted on as an afterthought.
  - **Secure Development Practices:** Follow secure coding practices, conduct regular code reviews, and use automated tools to detect and remediate security issues during development.
- **Economy of Mechanism:**
  - **Simplicity:** Keep the design as simple as possible while meeting security requirements. Complex systems are harder to understand, secure, and audit.

- **Avoid Overengineering:** Implement only the necessary security controls to meet the requirements, avoiding unnecessary complexity that could introduce new vulnerabilities.

- **Open Design:**
  - **Transparency:** Do not rely on security through obscurity. Instead, ensure that the security of the system does not depend on the secrecy of its design or implementation. Publicly known, well-vetted security algorithms and protocols should be used.
  - **Peer Review:** Encourage peer review and independent audits of the system's security design to identify and address potential weaknesses.
- **Compartmentalization:**
  - **Isolation:** Divide the system into isolated compartments that limit the impact of a breach in one component on the rest of the system. This can be achieved through techniques such as virtualization, containerization, or microservices.
  - **Sandboxing:** Run untrusted or less-trusted components in isolated environments (sandboxes) to prevent them from affecting other parts of the system.
- **Auditing and Monitoring:**
  - **Log Activities:** Implement comprehensive logging of user and system activities to detect and respond to suspicious behavior. Ensure that logs are protected against tampering.
  - **Regular Audits:** Conduct regular security audits and reviews of logs to identify potential security incidents and ensure compliance with security policies.

Applying Secure Design Principles with Threat Modeling

- **Combine Threat Modeling with Secure Design:** Use threat modeling insights to guide the application of secure design principles. For example, if threat modeling identifies a high risk of unauthorized access, apply the principle of least privilege and strong access controls to mitigate this risk.
- **Iterative Design:** Incorporate feedback from threat modeling into the design process, iteratively refining the system's architecture and controls to address identified threats.
- **Continuous Validation:** Throughout the SDLC, continuously validate that the secure design principles are being adhered to and that they effectively mitigate the identified threats.

Conclusion

Threat modeling and secure design principles are essential practices for building secure software. By systematically identifying and addressing potential threats early in the SDLC and applying well-established secure design principles, organizations can significantly reduce the risk of vulnerabilities and ensure that their systems are resilient against attacks. This proactive approach not only enhances the security of the software but also contributes to the overall quality, reliability, and trustworthiness of the final product.

Secure Coding Practices and Tools

Secure coding practices are essential for developing software that is resilient to security threats and vulnerabilities. By following best practices and using specialized tools, developers can minimize the risk of introducing security flaws into their code, thereby protecting applications from exploitation. Secure coding is a proactive approach that involves writing code with security in mind from the outset, rather than trying to fix security issues after they have been discovered.

Key Secure Coding Practices

Secure coding practices are guidelines and techniques that developers should follow to ensure that their code is secure. These practices are designed to prevent common vulnerabilities and to promote the development of robust, secure software.

Input Validation

- **Sanitize User Input:** Always validate and sanitize user inputs to ensure that they conform to expected formats. This prevents injection attacks, such as SQL injection, where an attacker could execute arbitrary code by exploiting improperly handled input.
- **Use Whitelisting:** Implement whitelisting (allowing only known good input) rather than blacklisting (blocking known bad input) to reduce the chances of malicious input being accepted.
- **Validate Input Length and Type:** Check that input data conforms to expected length and type constraints to prevent buffer overflows and type-related vulnerabilities.

Authentication and Access Control

- **Strong Authentication Mechanisms:** Use strong, multi-factor authentication (MFA) to verify the identity of users. Ensure that password policies require complex, unique passwords.
- **Principle of Least Privilege:** Assign the minimum necessary permissions to users and processes to perform their tasks. This reduces the potential damage that can occur if an account is compromised.
- **Secure Session Management:** Ensure that session tokens are securely generated, transmitted, and stored. Implement session expiration and re-authentication mechanisms to protect against session hijacking.

Error Handling and Logging

- **Graceful Error Handling:** Handle errors gracefully without exposing sensitive information, such as stack traces or database details, to end-users. Generic error messages should be presented to users, while detailed logs should be maintained for debugging and auditing.
- **Log Security-Relevant Events:** Implement logging for security-relevant events, such as failed login attempts, access control changes, and data access activities. Ensure that logs are securely stored and protected from tampering.
- **Avoid Logging Sensitive Data:** Be cautious about logging sensitive data, such as passwords or credit card numbers. If sensitive data must be logged, ensure it is properly encrypted.

Data Protection

- **Encryption:** Encrypt sensitive data both at rest and in transit to protect it from unauthorized access. Use strong, up-to-date encryption algorithms and manage encryption keys securely.
- **Secure Data Storage:** Store sensitive data, such as passwords and personal information, using secure storage mechanisms. For example, store passwords using a strong hash function with a salt to protect them from compromise.
- **Data Minimization:** Only collect and store the minimum amount of sensitive data necessary for the application to function. This reduces the impact of a potential data breach.

Secure Code Practices

- **Avoid Hardcoding Secrets:** Never hardcode secrets, such as passwords, API keys, or cryptographic keys, directly in the source code. Use secure vaults or environment variables to manage secrets.
- **Use Secure Libraries and Frameworks:** Leverage well-established, secure libraries and frameworks that have been vetted by the security community. Ensure that these libraries are regularly updated to address security vulnerabilities.
- **Regular Code Reviews:** Conduct regular peer code reviews with a focus on security. Having another set of eyes on the code can help catch security issues that the original developer might have missed.

Defense in Depth

- **Layered Security:** Implement multiple layers of security controls throughout the application to ensure that if one control fails, others remain in place to protect the system.
- **Input Validation at All Layers:** Ensure that input validation is performed at all layers of the application, including the client-side, server-side, and database.

Security Testing

- **Automated Security Testing:** Incorporate automated security testing tools into the development process to identify vulnerabilities early. These tools can perform static analysis, dynamic analysis, and dependency scanning.
- **Penetration Testing:** Conduct regular penetration testing to simulate attacks on the application and identify potential vulnerabilities. Use the results to improve the security of the codebase.

Tools for Secure Coding

Various tools are available to help developers write secure code by automatically detecting and mitigating potential security issues. These tools can be integrated into the development environment to provide continuous feedback and enforce secure coding practices.

Static Application Security Testing (SAST) Tools

SAST tools analyze source code, bytecode, or binaries for security vulnerabilities without executing the code. They are useful for detecting issues such as insecure coding patterns, buffer overflows, and improper error handling early in the development cycle.

Examples:

- **SonarQube:** An open-source platform that performs static analysis of code to identify bugs, vulnerabilities, and code smells. It supports multiple programming languages and integrates with CI/CD pipelines.
- **Checkmarx:** A commercial SAST tool that provides in-depth analysis of source code for a wide range of security vulnerabilities. It supports multiple languages and integrates with popular IDEs.
- **Veracode:** A cloud-based SAST solution that scans code for vulnerabilities and provides detailed remediation guidance. It supports multiple languages and integrates with CI/CD workflows.

Dynamic Application Security Testing (DAST) Tools

DAST tools analyze a running application to identify vulnerabilities by simulating attacks, such as SQL injection, cross-site scripting (XSS), and insecure session handling. These tools do not require access to the source code and are useful for testing applications in their deployed environments.

Examples:

- **OWASP ZAP (Zed Attack Proxy):** An open-source DAST tool that helps find security vulnerabilities in web applications. It is highly customizable and suitable for both manual and automated security testing.
- **Burp Suite:** A commercial tool widely used by security professionals for web application security testing. It includes automated scanning capabilities as well as tools for manual testing.
- **Acunetix:** A commercial DAST tool that automatically scans web applications for vulnerabilities, including SQL injection and XSS. It provides detailed reports and remediation suggestions.

Interactive Application Security Testing (IAST) Tools

IAST tools combine elements of SAST and DAST, providing real-time feedback on security vulnerabilities as the application runs. They integrate with the application during runtime, offering insights into how data flows through the system and identifying security issues within the context of the entire application.

Examples:

- **Contrast Security:** An IAST tool that continuously monitors applications in real-time to detect and report vulnerabilities as they are introduced. It integrates with CI/CD pipelines for continuous security monitoring.
- **Seeker by Synopsys:** An IAST tool that detects vulnerabilities by analyzing the interaction between code and runtime environment. It provides detailed insights into how vulnerabilities can be exploited and how to fix them.

Dependency Scanning Tools

Dependency scanning tools analyze the libraries and frameworks used in a project to identify known vulnerabilities. These tools are essential for managing the security of third-party components.

Examples:

- **OWASP Dependency-Check:** An open-source tool that scans project dependencies for known vulnerabilities. It supports multiple build systems and can generate detailed reports.
- **Snyk:** A commercial tool that scans open-source libraries and containers for known vulnerabilities. It provides automated fixes and integrates with CI/CD workflows.
- **NPM Audit:** A tool built into the Node.js package manager (NPM) that scans for vulnerabilities in Node.js project dependencies and suggests remediation steps.

Container Security Tools

For applications deployed in containers, container security tools are crucial for scanning container images and ensuring that they are free of vulnerabilities before deployment.

Examples:

- **Clair:** An open-source tool that scans Docker and OCI (Open Container Initiative) images for vulnerabilities. It integrates with container registries to automatically scan images upon upload.
- **Anchore Engine:** An open-source tool that performs deep image inspection and vulnerability scanning for Docker images. It integrates with CI/CD pipelines to enforce security policies.
- **Aqua Security:** A commercial solution that provides comprehensive container security, including image scanning, runtime protection, and network security for containerized environments.

Secure Development Environment Tools

Secure development environments provide tools and configurations that help developers adhere to secure coding practices while writing code.

Examples:

- **Visual Studio Code (VS Code) Extensions:** Various security extensions are available for VS Code, such as ESLint for enforcing coding standards and GitLens for managing secure code commits.
- **GitHub Advanced Security:** A set of features in GitHub that includes secret scanning, dependency review, and code scanning to help developers identify and fix security vulnerabilities within their repositories.

Code Review Tools

Code review tools facilitate peer reviews and automated analysis of code changes to ensure that security best practices are followed.

Examples:

- **Gerrit:** An open-source code review tool that integrates with Git repositories to facilitate code reviews and enforce security standards.
- **Crucible:** A commercial code review tool that allows teams to collaborate on code reviews and identify potential security issues early in the development process.
- **Phabricator:** An open-source suite of tools that includes a code review feature, enabling teams to conduct detailed reviews of code changes.

Integrating Secure Coding Practices into the SDLC

To be effective, secure coding practices and tools should be fully integrated into the SDLC. This integration ensures that security is considered at every stage of development, from planning through to deployment and maintenance.

Shift-Left Security

- **Early Detection:** Shift-left security involves moving security testing and validation earlier in the SDLC. By integrating SAST, dependency scanning, and other security tools into the development and build phases, vulnerabilities can be identified and addressed before they reach production.
- **Continuous Integration/Continuous Deployment (CI/CD):** Incorporate security testing into the CI/CD pipeline to ensure that every code change is automatically tested for security issues. This helps maintain a consistent security posture throughout the development process.

Security Champions

- **Empower Developers:** Identify and train security champions within the development team who can advocate for secure coding practices and act as a liaison between developers and security teams.
- **Ongoing Training:** Provide ongoing security training for developers to keep them informed about the latest threats, vulnerabilities, and secure coding techniques. This helps ensure that security is a core part of the development culture.

Collaboration Between Security and Development Teams

- **DevSecOps:** Foster a culture of collaboration between development, security, and operations teams (DevSecOps). This ensures that security

is integrated into every aspect of the software lifecycle, from development through to deployment and monitoring.
- **Cross-Functional Teams:** Create cross-functional teams that include members from development, security, and QA to ensure that security considerations are incorporated into every project decision.

Conclusion

Secure coding practices and tools are essential for developing robust, secure software that can withstand the ever-evolving threat landscape. By following best practices for input validation, authentication, error handling, data protection, and defense in depth, and by leveraging the right tools, developers can significantly reduce the risk of vulnerabilities in their code. Integrating these practices into the SDLC through shift-left security, continuous integration, and cross-functional collaboration ensures that security is an integral part of the development process, resulting in software that is secure by design.

Chapter 7

Managing Documented Information

Importance of Version Control and Secure Code Repositories

Version control and secure code repositories are fundamental components of modern software development. They provide a structured and secure way to manage code changes, collaborate among team members, and protect the integrity and confidentiality of the codebase. These practices are essential not only for the organization and efficiency of software projects but also for maintaining the security and quality of the software being developed.

What is Version Control?

Version control is the practice of tracking and managing changes to software code over time. It allows multiple developers to work on the same codebase simultaneously, tracks who made what changes, and provides the ability to revert to previous versions if necessary. Version control systems (VCS) like Git, Subversion (SVN), and Mercurial are commonly used to implement these practices.

Key Features of Version Control:

- **Branching and Merging:** Developers can create branches to work on different features or fixes independently and then merge their changes back into the main codebase.
- **History Tracking:** Every change made to the codebase is recorded, along with metadata such as who made the change, when it was made, and why (often via commit messages).
- **Collaboration:** Version control systems facilitate collaboration by allowing multiple developers to work on the same codebase simultaneously without overwriting each other's changes.
- **Reversion:** If a change introduces a bug or security vulnerability, version control allows the team to revert the codebase to a previous, stable version.

Importance of Version Control in Secure Software Development

Version control plays a critical role in secure software development for several reasons:

Accountability and Auditability:

- **Change Tracking:** Version control provides a complete history of changes made to the codebase, including who made each change and when. This accountability is crucial for security audits and for understanding the origin of security vulnerabilities.
- **Blame Functionality:** Most VCSs include a "blame" feature that identifies who last modified each line of code. This can be useful for tracing the source of a bug or vulnerability and for understanding the context of the change.

Collaboration with Security in Mind:

- **Secure Collaboration:** Version control systems enable developers to collaborate on code securely. They can create branches for feature development or bug fixes, allowing security teams to review changes before they are merged into the main codebase.
- **Code Reviews:** VCSs facilitate peer reviews of code changes, which are essential for identifying potential security issues. By integrating code review tools with version control, organizations can enforce secure coding practices.

Disaster Recovery and Integrity:

- **Backup and Recovery:** Version control systems act as a backup mechanism, ensuring that the codebase is not lost due to accidental deletion or corruption. If a security incident affects the codebase, the VCS can be used to restore it to a previous secure state.
- **Code Integrity:** By maintaining a history of changes, version control helps ensure the integrity of the codebase. Any unauthorized or unexpected changes can be identified and reverted.

Security During Development:

- **Isolated Development:** Developers can work on features or fixes in isolated branches, reducing the risk of introducing vulnerabilities into the main codebase. Changes can be tested and reviewed in isolation before being merged.
- **Controlled Access:** Version control systems typically integrate with access control mechanisms, ensuring that only authorized developers can make changes to certain parts of the codebase, thereby reducing the risk of unauthorized modifications.

Secure Code Repositories

A secure code repository is a version-controlled storage system where the source code is kept, managed, and accessed. Ensuring that code repositories are secure is critical to protecting the codebase from unauthorized access, tampering, and breaches.

Key Aspects of Secure Code Repositories:

- **Access Control:**
  - **Role-Based Access Control (RBAC):** Implement RBAC to restrict access to the code repository based on the role of the user. For example, some users may have read-only access, while others have write or admin privileges.
  - **Two-Factor Authentication (2FA):** Enforce 2FA for accessing code repositories to add an extra layer of security beyond just a username and password.
- **Encryption:**
  - **Data Encryption at Rest:** Ensure that the code stored in the repository is encrypted at rest, protecting it from unauthorized access or breaches.
  - **Encryption in Transit:** Use encrypted connections (e.g., HTTPS, SSH) for all communications with the repository to prevent interception and tampering during data transfer.
- **Regular Auditing and Monitoring:**
  - **Audit Logs:** Maintain audit logs of all access and changes to the repository. These logs should be reviewed regularly to detect any unauthorized access or suspicious activity.
  - **Automated Monitoring:** Use automated tools to monitor the repository for signs of unauthorized access or unusual patterns of activity that could indicate a security breach.
- **Secure Configuration:**
  - **Repository Configuration:** Ensure that the repository configuration settings are secure by default, limiting public access and enforcing strong authentication measures.
  - **Disable Default Accounts:** Remove or disable default accounts and credentials that could be exploited by attackers.
- **Compliance with Security Policies:**
  - **Policy Enforcement:** Enforce organizational security policies within the repository. This includes ensuring that only approved tools and libraries are used, and that all code meets security standards before being committed.

- o **Regular Security Reviews:** Conduct regular security reviews of the repository's configuration and access controls to ensure they meet current security best practices.

Version Control and Secure Repositories in DevOps:

- **Continuous Integration/Continuous Deployment (CI/CD):** Integrate version control and secure repositories with CI/CD pipelines to automate security testing and code deployment. This ensures that code is securely tested and deployed in a consistent manner.
- **Infrastructure as Code (IaC):** Secure code repositories are also critical for managing Infrastructure as Code (IaC). By storing IaC scripts in a secure repository, organizations can ensure that their infrastructure configurations are version-controlled, auditable, and protected from unauthorized changes.

Tools for Secure Code Repositories:

- **GitHub:** A popular platform for hosting Git repositories, GitHub offers security features such as 2FA, role-based access, and vulnerability alerts for project dependencies.
- **GitLab:** An integrated DevOps platform that includes Git repository hosting, GitLab provides features such as encrypted backups, audit logs, and built-in CI/CD capabilities.
- **Bitbucket:** A Git repository hosting service that integrates with Atlassian tools. Bitbucket offers access control, IP whitelisting, and 2FA to secure repositories.
- **Azure Repos:** Part of Microsoft Azure's DevOps services, Azure Repos provides secure Git repositories with fine-grained access controls, audit logs, and integration with Azure's security services.

Best Practices for Managing Version Control and Secure Repositories

To maximize the security and efficiency of version control and code repositories, organizations should follow these best practices:

Commit Hygiene:

- **Frequent, Small Commits:** Encourage developers to commit code frequently and in small increments. This makes it easier to track changes, review code, and identify issues.
- **Descriptive Commit Messages:** Require developers to write clear, descriptive commit messages that explain the purpose of the changes. This helps in understanding the history and context of the codebase.

Branch Management:

- **Use Branching Strategies:** Implement a branching strategy, such as Gitflow or feature branching, to manage the development workflow. This helps isolate changes, making it easier to manage and review code.
- **Regular Merging:** Regularly merge branches back into the main branch after thorough testing and review. This reduces the risk of long-lived branches diverging from the main codebase.

Repository Backup:

- **Regular Backups:** Ensure that repositories are regularly backed up to a secure, off-site location. This protects against data loss due to hardware failures, accidental deletion, or security incidents.
- **Disaster Recovery Plan:** Develop and test a disaster recovery plan that includes procedures for restoring repositories from backups in the event of a breach or other incident.

Security Scanning and Automation:

- **Automated Security Scanning:** Integrate automated security scanning tools into the version control process to detect vulnerabilities in code and dependencies before they are committed or merged.
- **CI/CD Integration:** Use CI/CD pipelines to automate security testing, code analysis, and deployment processes, ensuring that code is securely built, tested, and deployed.

Review and Update Security Practices:

- **Continuous Improvement:** Regularly review and update version control and repository management practices to adapt to new security threats and development methodologies.
- **Training and Awareness:** Provide ongoing training to developers on secure coding practices, version control best practices, and the importance of repository security.

Conclusion

Version control and secure code repositories are vital to maintaining the integrity, security, and efficiency of software development projects. By implementing robust version control practices and securing code repositories, organizations can protect their codebase from unauthorized access, ensure accountability, and facilitate secure collaboration among development teams. These practices not only enhance the security of the software but also contribute to better project management, traceability, and disaster recovery, ultimately leading to higher-quality, more secure software products.

Managing ISMS Documentation

Effective management of Information Security Management System (ISMS) documentation is essential for maintaining a robust and compliant information security framework. ISMS documentation serves as the foundation for establishing, implementing, operating, monitoring, reviewing, maintaining, and improving information security. Proper documentation ensures that security practices are consistently applied, provides a reference for audits and assessments, and helps demonstrate compliance with standards like ISO 27001:2022.

Importance of ISMS Documentation

ISMS documentation is critical for several reasons:

- **Compliance:** It provides evidence of compliance with ISO 27001:2022 and other relevant regulations and standards.
- **Consistency:** Ensures that information security practices are applied consistently across the organization.
- **Training and Awareness:** Acts as a resource for training employees on information security policies, procedures, and practices.
- **Audit Readiness:** Serves as a reference for internal and external audits, helping to demonstrate that the ISMS is effectively implemented and maintained.
- **Continuous Improvement:** Provides a basis for reviewing and improving information security processes.

Key Components of ISMS Documentation

ISMS documentation typically includes a range of documents that cover various aspects of information security management. The key components include:

Information Security Policy

- **Purpose:** The Information Security Policy outlines the organization's commitment to information security and provides high-level guidance on protecting information assets.
- **Content:** It includes the organization's security objectives, roles and responsibilities, scope of the ISMS, and the overall approach to managing information security risks.

- **Audience:** The policy is intended for all employees, contractors, and third parties who interact with the organization's information assets.

Risk Assessment and Risk Treatment Plan

- **Risk Assessment:** This document details the process of identifying, analyzing, and evaluating information security risks. It includes a risk register that tracks identified risks, their likelihood, impact, and overall risk rating.
- **Risk Treatment Plan:** Outlines the actions taken to mitigate identified risks, including the selection of security controls, implementation timelines, and responsibilities.

Statement of Applicability (SoA)

- **Purpose:** The SoA is a key document in ISO 27001:2022 compliance, listing all the security controls that have been selected to manage identified risks.
- **Content:** It includes justifications for including or excluding specific controls from the ISO 27001 Annex A, as well as a summary of how each control is implemented.
- **Audience:** The SoA is primarily used by the ISMS management team, auditors, and external assessors.

Information Security Objectives

- **Purpose:** Defines specific, measurable security goals that align with the organization's business objectives.
- **Content:** Includes security targets, metrics for measuring progress, and timelines for achieving objectives.
- **Audience:** Relevant to top management, ISMS management team, and other stakeholders involved in information security.

Security Procedures and Guidelines

- **Purpose:** Provide detailed instructions on how to implement specific security controls and manage information security risks.
- **Content:** May include procedures for access control, incident management, data encryption, secure software development, and more.
- **Audience:** Intended for IT and security teams, as well as any staff responsible for implementing and managing security controls.

Incident Response Plan

- **Purpose:** Outlines the procedures for detecting, reporting, and responding to information security incidents.
- **Content:** Includes roles and responsibilities, communication protocols, and steps for containment, eradication, recovery, and post-incident review.
- **Audience:** Relevant to the incident response team, IT staff, and management.

Training and Awareness Documentation

- **Purpose:** Ensures that all employees understand their roles in maintaining information security and are aware of the organization's security policies and procedures.
- **Content:** Includes training materials, records of training sessions, and awareness campaigns.
- **Audience:** All employees, contractors, and third parties.

Internal Audit and Management Review Reports

- **Purpose:** Document the results of internal audits and management reviews to assess the effectiveness of the ISMS and identify areas for improvement.
- **Content:** Includes audit findings, non-conformities, corrective actions, and recommendations for improvement.
- **Audience:** Used by the ISMS management team, top management, and auditors.

Records of Non-Conformities and Corrective Actions

- **Purpose:** Track non-conformities identified during audits or daily operations and document the corrective actions taken to address them.
- **Content:** Includes details of the non-conformity, root cause analysis, corrective actions, and verification of effectiveness.
- **Audience:** ISMS management team, auditors, and relevant stakeholders.

Best Practices for Managing ISMS Documentation

To effectively manage ISMS documentation, organizations should follow these best practices:

Document Control

- **Version Control:** Implement a version control system to track changes to ISMS documents. Each document should have a version number, date of the last update, and a history of changes.
- **Approval Workflow:** Establish a formal approval process for ISMS documents. Ensure that all documents are reviewed and approved by the appropriate stakeholders before they are published.
- **Document Retention:** Define retention periods for different types of ISMS documents, ensuring compliance with legal and regulatory requirements. Retain records for a sufficient period to support audits and investigations.

Accessibility and Security

- **Centralized Repository:** Store ISMS documents in a centralized, secure repository that is accessible to authorized personnel. This ensures that all stakeholders can easily access the latest versions of documents.
- **Access Controls:** Implement role-based access controls (RBAC) to restrict access to sensitive documents. Ensure that only authorized individuals can view, edit, or approve ISMS documentation.
- **Confidentiality:** Protect sensitive information within ISMS documents, such as security configurations, by applying appropriate encryption and access restrictions.

Regular Review and Updates

- **Scheduled Reviews:** Conduct regular reviews of ISMS documents to ensure they remain up-to-date and relevant. Schedule reviews based on document type, with policies and procedures typically reviewed annually.
- **Continuous Improvement:** Update documents as part of the continuous improvement process. Incorporate feedback from audits, incident reviews, and changes in the threat landscape.
- **Stakeholder Involvement:** Engage relevant stakeholders in the review process, including management, IT, and security teams, to ensure that documents reflect current practices and business needs.

Training and Awareness

- **Employee Training:** Provide regular training on ISMS documentation, ensuring that employees understand how to access and use the documents relevant to their roles.

- **Awareness Campaigns:** Run awareness campaigns to highlight important changes to ISMS documents and remind employees of their responsibilities under the ISMS.

Audit Preparation and Compliance

- **Audit Readiness:** Maintain ISMS documentation in a state that is ready for internal and external audits. Ensure that all required documents are up-to-date, complete, and easily accessible to auditors.
- **Compliance Tracking:** Use the ISMS documentation to track compliance with ISO 27001:2022 and other relevant standards. Regularly review documentation to identify gaps or areas of non-compliance.

Integration with Other Management Systems

- **Unified Documentation:** Where possible, integrate ISMS documentation with other management systems (e.g., quality management, IT service management) to reduce redundancy and improve consistency.
- **Cross-Referencing:** Cross-reference ISMS documents with related documents from other management systems to provide a comprehensive view of the organization's management practices.

Tools for Managing ISMS Documentation

Several tools can assist in managing ISMS documentation effectively:

Document Management Systems (DMS):

- **Microsoft SharePoint:** A widely used platform for managing and sharing documents, with built-in version control, approval workflows, and access controls.
- **Confluence:** A collaborative platform that allows teams to create, share, and manage documentation. It integrates with various tools and supports version control and permissions management.
- **Google Workspace:** Offers cloud-based document management with version control, access control, and collaboration features. It's suitable for organizations looking for a simple, scalable solution.

Compliance Management Tools:

- **VComply:** A platform for managing compliance-related documentation, including ISMS documents. It offers features for policy management, compliance tracking, and audit preparation.

- **ZenGRC:** A governance, risk, and compliance (GRC) tool that helps organizations manage ISMS documentation, track compliance with standards, and prepare for audits.
- **LogicGate:** A GRC software that enables organizations to manage risk, compliance, and ISMS documentation in a unified platform, with features for workflow automation and audit readiness.

Version Control Systems:

- **Git:** A distributed version control system that can be used for managing ISMS documents, especially when combined with platforms like GitHub, GitLab, or Bitbucket.
- **SVN (Subversion):** A centralized version control system that provides robust version tracking, access control, and document management capabilities.

Conclusion

Managing ISMS documentation is a critical task that requires careful planning, consistent practices, and the use of appropriate tools. By maintaining accurate, up-to-date, and secure documentation, organizations can ensure the effective operation of their ISMS, demonstrate compliance with ISO 27001:2022, and support continuous improvement in their information security practices. Proper documentation management not only helps protect the organization's information assets but also provides a solid foundation for training, auditing, and ongoing security management.

Audits and Compliance Tracking

Audits and compliance tracking are essential components of an effective Information Security Management System (ISMS). They ensure that an organization's security practices align with internal policies, industry standards, and regulatory requirements. Regular audits help identify gaps in the ISMS, provide insights for continuous improvement, and demonstrate the organization's commitment to information security. Compliance tracking, on the other hand, involves monitoring and documenting adherence to relevant standards and regulations, ensuring that the organization maintains its compliance status over time.

Importance of Audits in ISMS

Audits are systematic, independent evaluations of an organization's ISMS to determine whether it complies with established standards, policies, and procedures. They serve several critical functions:

- **Verification of Compliance:** Audits verify that the ISMS is in line with ISO 27001:2022 requirements, as well as other relevant standards and regulations.
- **Identification of Gaps:** Audits help identify weaknesses, non-conformities, and areas where security controls may be insufficient or ineffective.
- **Continuous Improvement:** The findings from audits provide actionable insights that organizations can use to improve their ISMS and strengthen their overall security posture.
- **Demonstrating Commitment:** Regular audits demonstrate to stakeholders, including customers, partners, and regulators, that the organization is committed to maintaining high standards of information security.

Types of Audits

There are several types of audits relevant to an ISMS:

- **Internal Audits:**
    - **Purpose:** Conducted by the organization's internal audit team or an independent internal party to assess the effectiveness of the ISMS.
    - **Frequency:** Typically conducted annually, but may be more frequent depending on the organization's needs and risk profile.

    - **Focus:** Internal audits focus on the organization's adherence to its own policies and procedures, as well as compliance with ISO 27001:2022 standards.
- **External Audits:**
    - **Purpose:** Conducted by an external, independent auditor to verify the organization's compliance with ISO 27001:2022 or other regulatory requirements.
    - **Frequency:** Often conducted annually or as required for certification purposes.
    - **Focus:** External audits provide an objective assessment of the ISMS and are necessary for achieving and maintaining ISO 27001 certification.
- **Surveillance Audits:**
    - **Purpose:** Conducted by certification bodies to ensure that the organization continues to meet the requirements of ISO 27001:2022 after initial certification.
    - **Frequency:** Typically conducted annually during the certification period (e.g., every three years).
    - **Focus:** Surveillance audits focus on verifying that the ISMS is still in place, effective, and continuously improving.
- **Regulatory Audits:**
    - **Purpose:** Conducted by regulatory bodies or commissioned third parties to ensure compliance with specific laws and regulations, such as GDPR, HIPAA, or PCI DSS.
    - **Frequency:** Frequency varies depending on regulatory requirements and the organization's risk profile.
    - **Focus:** Regulatory audits focus on compliance with legal and regulatory requirements, ensuring that the organization's practices align with applicable laws.

Audit Process

The audit process typically follows several key steps:

- **Planning:**
    - **Scope Definition:** Define the scope of the audit, including the specific areas, processes, and controls to be evaluated.
    - **Audit Schedule:** Develop a schedule for the audit, coordinating with relevant stakeholders to minimize disruption.
    - **Audit Criteria:** Establish the criteria against which the ISMS will be evaluated, such as ISO 27001:2022 standards, internal policies, and regulatory requirements.

- **Execution:**
  - **Data Collection:** Collect evidence to support the audit, such as documentation, records, logs, and interviews with personnel.
  - **Observation and Testing:** Observe practices and test controls to assess their effectiveness. This may involve reviewing logs, inspecting systems, and interviewing staff.
  - **Findings Documentation:** Document all findings, including any non-conformities, weaknesses, or areas for improvement.
- **Reporting:**
  - **Audit Report:** Prepare a comprehensive audit report that details the findings, including non-conformities, observations, and recommendations for corrective actions.
  - **Management Review:** Present the audit report to management for review and decision-making. Management should determine how to address the findings and implement corrective actions.
- **Follow-Up:**
  - **Corrective Actions:** Implement corrective actions to address identified non-conformities or weaknesses. These actions should be tracked and verified for effectiveness.
  - **Monitoring:** Continuously monitor the implementation of corrective actions and ensure that they effectively resolve the identified issues.
  - **Re-Audit (if necessary):** Conduct follow-up audits to verify that corrective actions have been successfully implemented and that the ISMS is now compliant.

Compliance Tracking

Compliance tracking involves the ongoing monitoring and documentation of the organization's adherence to applicable standards, regulations, and internal policies. It ensures that the organization remains compliant over time and that any deviations are promptly addressed.

Key Aspects of Compliance Tracking

- **Compliance Requirements Identification:**
  - **Legal and Regulatory Requirements:** Identify all relevant laws, regulations, and standards that apply to the organization. This may include ISO 27001:2022, GDPR, HIPAA, PCI DSS, and others.
  - **Internal Policies:** Track compliance with the organization's internal information security policies, procedures, and guidelines.

- **Documentation and Record-Keeping:**
    - **Compliance Documentation:** Maintain detailed records of compliance activities, including audit reports, training records, risk assessments, and corrective actions.
    - **Version Control:** Use version control to track changes to compliance documentation and ensure that the most current versions are always available.
- **Monitoring and Reporting:**
    - **Continuous Monitoring:** Implement tools and processes for continuous monitoring of compliance with security controls and policies. This may include automated tools for monitoring access controls, data protection measures, and system configurations.
    - **Compliance Dashboard:** Use a compliance dashboard to track and visualize compliance status across the organization. Dashboards can provide real-time insights into areas of non-compliance and help prioritize corrective actions.
- **Compliance Audits and Assessments:**
    - **Regular Assessments:** Conduct regular internal compliance assessments to verify adherence to standards and regulations. These assessments should be aligned with the audit schedule.
    - **Third-Party Assessments:** Engage third-party assessors or auditors to conduct independent assessments of compliance, especially for regulatory requirements.
- **Corrective Actions and Improvement:**
    - **Non-Conformity Management:** Track and manage non-conformities identified during audits and assessments. Implement corrective actions promptly to resolve issues.
    - **Continuous Improvement:** Use compliance tracking as a tool for continuous improvement. Regularly review compliance status and identify opportunities to enhance security practices.
- **Training and Awareness:**
    - **Compliance Training:** Provide regular training to employees on compliance requirements, including updates to regulations, standards, and internal policies.
    - **Awareness Programs:** Run awareness programs to keep employees informed about the importance of compliance and their role in maintaining it.

Tools for Compliance Tracking

Several tools can assist in managing audits and compliance tracking:

- **GRC Platforms (Governance, Risk, and Compliance):**
  - **RSA Archer:** A comprehensive GRC platform that helps organizations manage risk, compliance, and audit activities. It provides tools for compliance tracking, audit management, and reporting.
  - **MetricStream:** A GRC solution that offers modules for compliance management, audit management, and risk management. It helps organizations track compliance with regulations and internal policies.
  - **SAP GRC:** A suite of tools for managing governance, risk, and compliance activities. It includes features for compliance monitoring, risk assessment, and audit management.
- **Compliance Management Systems:**
  - **VComply:** A platform designed for managing compliance requirements, including ISO 27001:2022 and other standards. It provides tools for tracking compliance, managing policies, and preparing for audits.
  - **ZenGRC:** A GRC tool that simplifies compliance tracking, audit preparation, and risk management. It offers features for tracking compliance with multiple frameworks, including ISO 27001.

- **Audit Management Tools:**
  - **AuditBoard:** An audit management platform that helps organizations manage audit processes, track findings, and implement corrective actions. It integrates with compliance tracking to provide a unified view of audit and compliance activities.
  - **TeamMate:** An audit management tool that streamlines the audit process, from planning and execution to reporting and follow-up. It helps organizations manage audit workflows and track compliance.

Compliance Reporting and Communication

- **Regular Reporting:** Generate regular compliance reports for management, stakeholders, and regulators. Reports should provide an overview of compliance status, audit findings, and corrective actions.
- **Management Communication:** Ensure that compliance status and audit findings are regularly communicated to top management.

Management should be involved in decision-making regarding corrective actions and improvements.

Continuous Improvement Through Audits and Compliance Tracking

Audits and compliance tracking should be seen as tools for continuous improvement, not just for maintaining compliance. By regularly reviewing audit findings and compliance status, organizations can identify trends, address recurring issues, and enhance their ISMS over time.

- **Feedback Loops:** Establish feedback loops between audit results, compliance tracking, and ISMS improvements. Use insights gained from audits to refine policies, procedures, and controls.
- **Adaptive Compliance:** Stay informed about changes in regulations and standards, and adapt the ISMS to meet new requirements. Regularly update compliance tracking tools and processes to reflect these changes.
- **Proactive Risk Management:** Use compliance tracking data to proactively manage risks. Identify areas where compliance may be at risk and take preventive actions to avoid non-conformities.

Conclusion

Audits and compliance tracking are essential components of an effective ISMS, ensuring that the organization's information security practices meet regulatory requirements and industry standards. By conducting regular audits, tracking compliance continuously, and using the insights gained to drive improvements, organizations can maintain a robust security posture, reduce the risk of non-compliance, and demonstrate their commitment to information security. Leveraging appropriate tools and technologies further enhances the efficiency and effectiveness of these processes, enabling organizations to manage compliance proactively and responsively.

Chapter 8
Vulnerability and Incident Management

Strategies for Effective Vulnerability Management

Vulnerability management is a critical aspect of an organization's information security strategy. It involves identifying, evaluating, prioritizing, and remediating security vulnerabilities in software, hardware, and network systems. Effective vulnerability management helps protect the organization from security breaches, data loss, and operational disruptions by ensuring that vulnerabilities are addressed before they can be exploited by attackers.

Understanding Vulnerability Management

Vulnerability management is an ongoing process that requires continuous monitoring, assessment, and remediation efforts. It typically involves the following key activities:

- **Identification:** Discovering vulnerabilities through automated scans, manual testing, threat intelligence, and reports from vendors or researchers.
- **Assessment:** Evaluating the severity and potential impact of each identified vulnerability to determine the appropriate response.
- **Prioritization:** Ranking vulnerabilities based on factors such as severity, exploitability, and the criticality of the affected assets.
- **Remediation:** Applying patches, configuring security controls, or implementing other measures to mitigate or eliminate the vulnerability.
- **Verification:** Ensuring that remediation actions are successful and that vulnerabilities are no longer present.
- **Reporting and Documentation:** Maintaining records of identified vulnerabilities, remediation efforts, and the current status of vulnerabilities within the organization.

Key Strategies for Effective Vulnerability Management

To manage vulnerabilities effectively, organizations should adopt a systematic approach that incorporates the following strategies:

Implement a Comprehensive Vulnerability Management Program

- **Establish Clear Policies and Procedures:** Develop and document a vulnerability management policy that outlines the roles, responsibilities, and processes involved in managing vulnerabilities. Ensure that all stakeholders are aware of and understand these policies.

- **Define Scope:** Clearly define the scope of the vulnerability management program, including the systems, applications, and networks that will be monitored. Consider including third-party software and cloud-based services in the scope.

Conduct Regular Vulnerability Scanning

- **Automated Scanning:** Use automated vulnerability scanning tools to regularly scan systems, networks, and applications for known vulnerabilities. These tools can identify weaknesses such as outdated software, misconfigurations, and missing patches.

  Examples of Vulnerability Scanning Tools:
  - **Nessus:** A widely used vulnerability scanner that identifies vulnerabilities across a variety of systems and devices.
  - **QualysGuard:** A cloud-based scanner that provides comprehensive coverage of vulnerabilities and compliance issues.
  - **OpenVAS:** An open-source tool that offers a broad range of vulnerability scanning capabilities.
- **Authenticated Scans:** Perform authenticated scans where possible, as these provide deeper visibility into system configurations and vulnerabilities that may not be detectable through unauthenticated scans.
- **Frequency of Scans:** Schedule scans on a regular basis—such as weekly or monthly—and after significant changes to the IT environment, such as the deployment of new systems or applications.

Prioritize Vulnerabilities Based on Risk

- **Use Risk-Based Prioritization:** Prioritize vulnerabilities based on their potential impact on the organization. Factors to consider include:
  - **CVSS Scores:** Use the Common Vulnerability Scoring System (CVSS) to evaluate the severity of vulnerabilities. Higher CVSS scores indicate more critical vulnerabilities.
  - **Business Impact:** Assess the potential impact of a vulnerability on the organization's critical assets, such as customer data, financial systems, or intellectual property.
  - **Exploit Availability:** Consider whether there are known exploits or active threats targeting the vulnerability. Vulnerabilities with available exploits should be prioritized for remediation.

    - **Asset Criticality:** Prioritize vulnerabilities on systems and applications that are critical to business operations, as their compromise could lead to significant disruptions.

Implement Effective Remediation Strategies

- **Patch Management:** Establish a robust patch management process to ensure that software and systems are kept up to date with the latest security patches. Automate patch deployment where possible to reduce the time between patch release and implementation.
  Patch Testing: Before deploying patches, test them in a controlled environment to ensure they do not introduce new issues or disrupt business operations.
- **Configuration Management:** Regularly review and harden system configurations to reduce the attack surface. Implement security best practices, such as disabling unnecessary services, changing default passwords, and enforcing secure protocols.
- **Mitigation and Workarounds:** For vulnerabilities that cannot be patched immediately, implement temporary mitigation measures or workarounds. This may include disabling vulnerable services, restricting network access, or applying additional security controls.

Continuous Monitoring and Threat Intelligence Integration

- **Continuous Monitoring:** Implement continuous monitoring to detect new vulnerabilities as they arise. This includes real-time monitoring of systems, networks, and applications for signs of exploitation or compromise.
- **Threat Intelligence:** Integrate threat intelligence feeds into the vulnerability management process to stay informed about emerging threats and vulnerabilities. This helps prioritize vulnerabilities that are actively being exploited in the wild.
    - **Threat Intelligence Platforms:** Use platforms like MISP (Malware Information Sharing Platform) or commercial solutions to gather, analyze, and share threat intelligence data.

Foster Collaboration Across Teams

- **Cross-Functional Collaboration:** Encourage collaboration between security, IT, and development teams to ensure vulnerabilities are addressed effectively. Security teams can identify vulnerabilities, while IT and development teams are responsible for implementing fixes.

- **DevSecOps Integration:** Integrate vulnerability management into the DevSecOps pipeline to identify and remediate vulnerabilities early in the development process. This approach reduces the risk of introducing vulnerabilities into production environments.

Regularly Review and Improve the Vulnerability Management Process

- **Post-Remediation Verification:** After vulnerabilities are remediated, verify that the actions taken were successful and that the vulnerabilities are no longer present. This may involve re-scanning systems or conducting manual tests.
- **Root Cause Analysis:** For significant vulnerabilities or recurring issues, perform root cause analysis to identify underlying problems and prevent similar vulnerabilities from occurring in the future.
- **Continuous Improvement:** Regularly review and update the vulnerability management program to incorporate lessons learned, address new threats, and align with changes in the IT environment.

Reporting and Documentation

- **Maintain Detailed Records:** Document all aspects of the vulnerability management process, including identified vulnerabilities, assessment results, remediation actions, and verification outcomes. This documentation is critical for audits and compliance reporting.
- **Regular Reporting:** Provide regular reports to management and stakeholders on the status of vulnerability management activities. Reports should include metrics such as the number of vulnerabilities identified, time to remediation, and the status of high-priority vulnerabilities.
- **Compliance Tracking:** Ensure that the vulnerability management process meets regulatory and industry compliance requirements, such as those specified by ISO 27001, PCI DSS, or HIPAA.

Tools for Effective Vulnerability Management

There are several tools available to support each phase of the vulnerability management process. These tools can automate scanning, prioritize vulnerabilities, and track remediation efforts:

- **Vulnerability Scanners:**
    - **Nessus:** Provides comprehensive scanning for network vulnerabilities, including configuration issues, outdated software, and missing patches.

    - **QualysGuard:** Offers cloud-based scanning for networks, applications, and web services, with integrated compliance management features.
    - **OpenVAS:** An open-source vulnerability scanner with a wide range of capabilities, including network scanning, configuration checks, and vulnerability assessment.
- **Patch Management Tools:**
    - **Microsoft SCCM (System Center Configuration Manager):** A tool for managing and deploying patches across Windows environments.
    - **Ivanti Patch Management:** Provides patch management for both Windows and third-party applications, with automated deployment features.
    - **SolarWinds Patch Manager:** Automates patch management for Microsoft and third-party applications, with extensive reporting and compliance tracking capabilities.
- **Threat Intelligence Platforms:**
    - **MISP:** An open-source threat intelligence platform that facilitates the sharing of threat information among organizations.
    - **Recorded Future:** A commercial threat intelligence platform that provides real-time threat data and analysis for proactive vulnerability management.
- **Vulnerability Management Platforms:**
    - **Rapid7 InsightVM:** A vulnerability management solution that integrates scanning, prioritization, and remediation tracking with threat intelligence.
    - **Tenable.io:** A cloud-based platform that provides comprehensive vulnerability management, including asset discovery, scanning, and risk-based prioritization.
    - **Qualys VMDR (Vulnerability Management Detection and Response):** An integrated platform for managing the entire vulnerability lifecycle, from detection to remediation and response.

Conclusion

Effective vulnerability management is essential for protecting an organization's information assets from security threats. By implementing a comprehensive vulnerability management program, conducting regular scans, prioritizing vulnerabilities based on risk, and fostering collaboration across teams, organizations can significantly reduce their exposure to security risks. Continuous monitoring, integration of threat intelligence, and ongoing improvement of the vulnerability management process ensure that the organization remains resilient against emerging threats and vulnerabilities.

Incident Response Planning and Execution

Incident response planning and execution are critical components of an organization's cybersecurity strategy. A well-developed incident response plan (IRP) enables an organization to effectively detect, respond to, and recover from security incidents, minimizing the impact on operations, data integrity, and reputation. The key to successful incident response lies in preparation, clear communication, and rapid, coordinated action.

Importance of Incident Response Planning

Incident response planning is essential for several reasons:

- **Minimizing Impact:** A well-prepared response can reduce the damage caused by a security incident, including financial loss, data breaches, and operational disruptions.
- **Ensuring Compliance:** Many regulations and standards, such as GDPR, HIPAA, and ISO 27001, require organizations to have a formal incident response plan in place.
- **Maintaining Business Continuity:** Effective incident response helps maintain business operations during and after a security incident, minimizing downtime and service disruptions.
- **Protecting Reputation:** A timely and transparent response to a security incident can help maintain customer trust and protect the organization's reputation.

Key Components of an Incident Response Plan

An effective incident response plan should include the following key components:

Incident Response Policy

- **Purpose:** The policy outlines the organization's commitment to incident response, establishes the scope, and defines the roles and responsibilities of the incident response team (IRT).
- **Scope:** Define the types of incidents covered by the plan, such as data breaches, denial-of-service attacks, malware infections, insider threats, and more.

- **Roles and Responsibilities:** Clearly define the roles of the incident response team members, including the incident manager, security analysts, communication officers, legal advisors, and IT staff.

Incident Response Team (IRT)

- **Team Structure:** The IRT should include individuals with expertise in IT, cybersecurity, legal, communications, and business operations. The team should be cross-functional to address the various aspects of incident response.
- **Contact Information:** Maintain an up-to-date contact list for all IRT members, including primary and secondary points of contact.
- **Training and Drills:** Regularly train the IRT on their roles and responsibilities, and conduct incident response drills (e.g., tabletop exercises) to ensure preparedness.

Incident Response Phases

Incident response typically follows a structured process consisting of several phases:

Preparation

- **Incident Detection Tools:** Implement tools for detecting security incidents, such as intrusion detection systems (IDS), security information and event management (SIEM) systems, and antivirus software.
- **Baseline Security Posture:** Establish a baseline for normal network and system behavior to detect anomalies that may indicate a security incident.
- **IRP Documentation:** Develop and maintain detailed documentation of the incident response plan, including procedures, checklists, and templates.

Identification

- **Incident Detection:** Monitor systems, networks, and applications for signs of security incidents. This may involve automated alerts from security tools or reports from employees or third parties.
- **Incident Triage:** Assess the nature and scope of the detected incident to determine its severity and potential impact. Categorize incidents based on predefined criteria (e.g., critical, high, medium, low).
- **Initial Reporting:** Document the initial findings and notify the IRT to initiate the response process.

Containment

- **Short-Term Containment:** Implement immediate actions to prevent the incident from spreading or causing further damage. This may include isolating affected systems, disabling compromised accounts, or blocking malicious IP addresses.
- **Long-Term Containment:** Develop and execute a strategy to contain the incident while maintaining business operations. This may involve applying patches, reconfiguring network segments, or setting up temporary systems.

Eradication

- **Root Cause Analysis:** Identify the root cause of the incident to ensure it is fully addressed. This may involve analyzing malware, reviewing logs, or conducting forensic investigations.
- **Removing the Threat:** Eliminate the threat by removing malicious software, closing vulnerabilities, and applying security patches. Ensure that all remnants of the attack are completely eradicated.

Recovery

- **System Restoration:** Restore affected systems and data to normal operations, using backups if necessary. Ensure that restored systems are free from vulnerabilities and fully secure.
- **Monitoring for Recurrence:** Monitor the systems closely after recovery to detect any signs of the threat re-emerging. This may involve increased logging, heightened network monitoring, or regular scans.
- **Validation:** Validate the integrity of the restored systems and confirm that they are functioning correctly.

Lessons Learned

- **Post-Incident Review:** Conduct a thorough review of the incident, including how it was detected, the effectiveness of the response, and the impact on the organization.
- **Report Preparation:** Prepare a detailed incident report that documents the timeline of events, actions taken, and the root cause analysis. Include recommendations for improving the incident response process.
- **Process Improvement:** Use the insights gained from the incident to update and improve the incident response plan, policies, and security controls. Conduct training sessions to address any gaps identified during the incident.

Communication Plan

- **Internal Communication:** Establish protocols for communicating with internal stakeholders, including management, IT staff, and affected departments. Ensure that communication is clear, timely, and coordinated.
- **External Communication:** Develop a strategy for communicating with external stakeholders, such as customers, partners, regulators, and the media. Ensure that the communication is consistent, transparent, and complies with legal requirements.
- **Crisis Management:** Designate a crisis management team to handle public relations and media inquiries. Ensure that all external communications are approved by this team to maintain consistency.

Legal and Regulatory Considerations

- **Compliance Requirements:** Ensure that the incident response plan addresses all relevant legal and regulatory requirements, such as breach notification laws, data protection regulations (e.g., GDPR), and industry standards (e.g., PCI DSS).
- **Legal Counsel:** Include legal advisors in the IRT to provide guidance on regulatory obligations, contractual responsibilities, and potential legal risks.
- **Breach Notification:** Develop a procedure for notifying affected individuals, regulators, and other stakeholders in the event of a data breach. Ensure that the notification process complies with legal timelines and content requirements.

Documentation and Reporting

- **Incident Documentation:** Maintain detailed records of all actions taken during the incident response process, including timelines, communications, and decisions. This documentation is essential for legal, regulatory, and audit purposes.
- **Reporting Templates:** Develop standardized templates for incident reports, including incident summary, impact assessment, root cause analysis, and corrective actions.
- **Audit Trail:** Ensure that all incident response activities are logged and can be audited. This includes maintaining logs of communications, decisions, and actions taken during the response.

Tools for Incident Response

Several tools can assist in various stages of incident response, from detection to recovery:

- **SIEM (Security Information and Event Management):**
  - **Splunk:** A powerful SIEM platform that collects and analyzes security data from multiple sources to detect and respond to incidents.
  - **IBM QRadar:** A comprehensive SIEM solution that provides real-time threat detection, incident analysis, and automated response capabilities.
- **Endpoint Detection and Response (EDR):**
  - **CrowdStrike Falcon:** An EDR tool that provides advanced threat detection, incident response, and endpoint protection.
  - **Carbon Black:** An EDR platform that offers real-time visibility into endpoint activity, threat hunting, and incident response capabilities.
- **Forensic Analysis Tools:**
  - **FTK (Forensic Toolkit):** A digital forensics tool used for collecting, analyzing, and reporting on digital evidence during an incident investigation.
  - **EnCase:** A widely used forensic analysis tool that helps investigators identify, preserve, and analyze digital evidence.
- **Incident Response Platforms:**
  - **TheHive:** An open-source incident response platform that helps manage and track security incidents through their lifecycle.
  - **Cortex XSOAR:** A Security Orchestration, Automation, and Response (SOAR) platform that integrates with various security tools to automate and coordinate incident response activities.

Testing and Updating the Incident Response Plan

An incident response plan should be regularly tested and updated to ensure its effectiveness:

Testing

- **Tabletop Exercises:** Conduct tabletop exercises where the IRT walks through simulated incident scenarios to test their response and decision-making processes.
- **Live Drills:** Perform live incident response drills that simulate real-world attacks to evaluate the readiness of the IRT and the effectiveness of the incident response plan.

- **Red Team/Blue Team Exercises:** Engage in red team/blue team exercises where one team simulates an attack (red team) and the other team defends against it (blue team). This helps identify weaknesses in the incident response process.

Updating the Plan

- **Post-Incident Updates:** After each incident, review the incident response plan and update it based on lessons learned. Address any gaps or weaknesses identified during the incident.
- **Regular Reviews:** Conduct regular reviews of the incident response plan, at least annually or after significant changes in the organization's environment, such as new technologies or regulatory requirements.
- **Stakeholder Feedback:** Involve stakeholders in the review process to ensure that the plan remains relevant and aligned with business objectives.

Conclusion

Incident response planning and execution are essential for protecting an organization from the potentially devastating effects of security incidents. A well-prepared incident response plan enables rapid, coordinated, and effective action, minimizing the impact on business operations, data integrity, and reputation. By continuously refining the plan, conducting regular training and exercises, and leveraging appropriate tools, organizations can enhance their resilience and ensure that they are ready to respond to any security incident that may arise.

Post-Incident Reviews and Continual Improvement

Post-incident reviews (PIRs) are a critical component of an effective incident response strategy, serving as a key mechanism for learning from security incidents and driving continual improvement in an organization's security posture. By systematically analyzing incidents after they occur, organizations can identify root causes, assess the effectiveness of their response, and implement improvements to prevent similar incidents in the future. This process not only strengthens the organization's ability to handle future incidents but also supports the overall resilience and maturity of its Information Security Management System (ISMS).

Importance of Post-Incident Reviews

Post-incident reviews are essential for several reasons:

- **Learning from Incidents:** PIRs provide valuable insights into what went wrong during an incident and how similar issues can be avoided in the future.
- **Improving Response Effectiveness:** By evaluating the incident response process, organizations can identify areas for improvement and make necessary adjustments to enhance the speed and effectiveness of future responses.
- **Root Cause Analysis:** PIRs help identify the underlying causes of incidents, enabling the organization to address the root issues rather than just the symptoms.
- **Compliance and Accountability:** Conducting PIRs demonstrates the organization's commitment to security and continuous improvement, which is often required by regulatory standards such as ISO 27001, GDPR, and HIPAA.
- **Enhancing Security Posture:** The findings from PIRs contribute to the ongoing improvement of security policies, procedures, and controls, thereby strengthening the overall security posture of the organization.

Conducting an Effective Post-Incident Review

An effective post-incident review involves several key steps:

Gather the Incident Response Team

- **Involve All Relevant Parties:** Ensure that all members of the incident response team (IRT) who were involved in the incident are present for the review. This may include security analysts, IT staff, legal advisors, communications personnel, and management.
- **Encourage Open Discussion:** Foster an environment where team members feel comfortable sharing their experiences and insights without fear of blame. The goal is to learn and improve, not to assign blame.

Review the Incident Timeline

- **Chronological Analysis:** Create a detailed timeline of the incident, from the initial detection to the final resolution. This should include key events, actions taken, and decisions made during the response.
- **Identify Key Milestones:** Highlight critical points in the incident response process, such as when the incident was detected, when containment measures were implemented, and when recovery was completed.
- **Assess Communication:** Review the effectiveness of communication throughout the incident, both within the IRT and with external stakeholders. Identify any communication breakdowns or delays that may have impacted the response.

Perform Root Cause Analysis

- **Identify Root Causes:** Determine the underlying causes of the incident, such as vulnerabilities, misconfigurations, human errors, or process failures. This analysis should go beyond the immediate cause of the incident to identify systemic issues.
- **Use Structured Techniques:** Consider using structured techniques like the "5 Whys" or Fishbone (Ishikawa) diagrams to systematically explore the root causes of the incident.

Evaluate the Incident Response Process

- **Assess Response Effectiveness:** Evaluate how well the incident response plan was executed. Consider factors such as the speed of detection, the effectiveness of containment and eradication measures, and the efficiency of the recovery process.

- **Identify Gaps and Weaknesses:** Identify any gaps or weaknesses in the incident response process, such as delays in detection, inadequate containment strategies, or insufficient resources. Determine whether the incident response plan needs to be updated based on these findings.

Document Lessons Learned

- **Capture Key Insights:** Document the key lessons learned from the incident, including what went well and what could have been done better. Focus on actionable insights that can be applied to improve future incident response efforts.
- **Incorporate Feedback:** Include feedback from all IRT members and relevant stakeholders to ensure that the review captures a comprehensive view of the incident and response.

Develop an Action Plan for Improvement

- **Recommend Improvements:** Based on the findings from the PIR, develop a set of recommendations for improving the incident response process, security controls, and overall security posture.
- **Prioritize Actions:** Prioritize the recommended improvements based on their potential impact and feasibility. Focus on addressing the most critical gaps first.
- **Assign Responsibilities:** Assign specific responsibilities for implementing the recommended improvements. Ensure that each action item has a clear owner and timeline for completion.

Communicate the Findings

- **Internal Communication:** Share the findings and action plan with relevant stakeholders within the organization, including management, IT, and security teams. Ensure that everyone understands the lessons learned and the steps being taken to improve.
- **External Reporting:** If the incident was significant or involved regulatory requirements, prepare a report for external stakeholders, such as customers, partners, or regulators. Ensure that the report is clear, transparent, and aligned with any legal obligations.

Continuous Improvement Through Post-Incident Reviews

Post-incident reviews are a key driver of continuous improvement in an organization’s security posture. The following strategies can help ensure that PIRs lead to meaningful and sustained improvements:

Update the Incident Response Plan

- **Incorporate Lessons Learned:** Use the findings from PIRs to update the incident response plan (IRP), making it more effective for future incidents. This may involve revising procedures, updating contact lists, or enhancing communication protocols.
- **Test the Updated Plan:** After making updates to the IRP, conduct tabletop exercises or live drills to test the changes and ensure that the team is familiar with the new procedures.

Enhance Security Controls

- **Implement Remediations:** Address the root causes of the incident by implementing the recommended security controls, patches, or process changes. Ensure that these remediations are tested and validated.
- **Strengthen Preventative Measures:** Use the insights from PIRs to strengthen preventative security measures, such as improving vulnerability management, enhancing monitoring and detection capabilities, or providing additional training to employees.

Foster a Culture of Continuous Improvement

- **Encourage Learning:** Promote a culture of continuous improvement where lessons from incidents are actively used to improve security practices. Encourage employees to share insights and suggestions for enhancing security.
- **Regular Reviews:** Conduct regular post-incident reviews, even for minor incidents, to build a habit of learning and improvement. Over time, this practice will lead to a more resilient security posture.

Monitor and Measure Progress

- **Track Improvement Actions:** Use metrics and KPIs to track the implementation of recommended improvements and measure their effectiveness. This helps ensure that the organization is making tangible progress in enhancing its security posture.
- **Regular Reporting:** Provide regular reports to management on the status of improvement actions and the overall effectiveness of the incident response process. Highlight successes and areas where further improvement is needed.

Review and Update Related Policies and Procedures

- **Align with Lessons Learned:** Review and update related security policies and procedures based on the findings from PIRs. Ensure that all relevant documentation reflects the changes and improvements made.

- **Integrate with Other Management Systems:** Consider how the lessons learned from security incidents can inform other management systems, such as risk management, business continuity, and compliance. This holistic approach helps strengthen the organization's overall governance framework.

Tools for Post-Incident Reviews

Several tools can assist in conducting effective post-incident reviews and supporting continuous improvement:

- **Incident Response Platforms:**
  - **TheHive:** An open-source incident response platform that helps manage and document security incidents, including post-incident reviews.
  - **Cortex XSOAR:** A Security Orchestration, Automation, and Response (SOAR) platform that integrates with various security tools to automate incident response and track post-incident actions.
- **Root Cause Analysis Tools:**
  - **Fishbone Diagram (Ishikawa):** A tool for identifying and categorizing the root causes of incidents, often used in post-incident reviews.
  - **5 Whys:** A simple but effective technique for identifying the root cause of an issue by asking "Why?" repeatedly until the underlying cause is found.
- **Collaboration and Documentation Tools:**
  - **Confluence:** A collaborative platform for documenting post-incident reviews, action plans, and lessons learned. It provides templates and version control for managing documentation.
  - **Microsoft Teams/Slack:** Communication and collaboration tools that can be used to coordinate post-incident review meetings and share findings with the team.

Conclusion

Post-incident reviews and continual improvement are critical for maintaining and enhancing an organization's security posture. By systematically analyzing incidents, identifying root causes, and implementing actionable improvements, organizations can reduce the likelihood of future incidents and improve their ability to respond effectively. A culture of continuous improvement, supported by regular

PIRs and the integration of lessons learned into security practices, ensures that the organization remains resilient in the face of evolving threats.

Part 5

Cultivating a Security-First Culture

Chapter 9

Competence and Training

Developing Secure Coding Skills Among Developers

Ensuring that developers possess strong secure coding skills is critical to creating robust, secure software. By integrating security into the development process from the start, organizations can significantly reduce vulnerabilities and enhance the overall security posture of their applications. Developing these skills involves a combination of education, hands-on practice, and continuous learning.

Importance of Secure Coding

Secure coding is the practice of writing software code that is resistant to security threats and vulnerabilities. It is a proactive approach to preventing common security issues, such as SQL injection, cross-site scripting (XSS), and buffer overflows, which can be exploited by attackers. The benefits of secure coding include:

- **Reducing Vulnerabilities:** Secure coding practices help minimize the risk of security flaws that can be exploited by attackers.
- **Protecting Data Integrity:** By ensuring that code is secure, developers can protect sensitive data from unauthorized access, modification, or deletion.
- **Complying with Standards:** Many regulatory frameworks and industry standards, such as PCI DSS, HIPAA, and ISO 27001, require organizations to implement secure coding practices.
- **Building Customer Trust:** Secure software enhances customer confidence and trust, as it reduces the likelihood of data breaches and other security incidents.

Strategies for Developing Secure Coding Skills

To effectively develop secure coding skills among developers, organizations should implement a structured approach that includes education, hands-on practice, and continuous improvement.

Provide Secure Coding Training

- **Foundational Training:** Offer foundational secure coding training to all developers, covering essential topics such as input validation, authentication, authorization, error handling, and data protection.

Topics to Cover:

- Common vulnerabilities and their prevention (e.g., SQL injection, XSS, CSRF)
- Secure coding principles (e.g., least privilege, defense in depth)
- Secure software development lifecycle (SDLC) practices
- Best practices for secure coding in specific programming languages (e.g., Java, Python, JavaScript)

- **Advanced Training:** Provide advanced training for senior developers or those working on high-risk projects. This training should delve deeper into secure design patterns, threat modeling, cryptography, and secure architecture.

  Example Courses:
  - OWASP Top Ten and how to avoid these vulnerabilities
  - Secure development frameworks and libraries
  - Secure DevOps practices (DevSecOps)
- **Continuous Learning:** Encourage continuous learning by providing access to online courses, webinars, security conferences, and certifications (e.g., CSSLP, CEH) that focus on secure coding.

Hands-On Practice and Simulation

- **Code Reviews and Peer Learning:** Implement regular code reviews with a focus on security. Peer reviews help developers learn from each other's experiences and catch security issues early in the development process.

  Structured Code Review Process:
  - Establish a checklist of security considerations for code reviews.
  - Include security champions in the review process to provide specialized expertise.
  - Use tools to automate parts of the review, but ensure human oversight for complex security issues.
- **Capture the Flag (CTF) Challenges:** Organize or participate in Capture the Flag challenges that focus on secure coding. These challenges simulate real-world security scenarios and encourage developers to practice identifying and fixing vulnerabilities in a controlled environment.

  Popular CTF Platforms:
  - **Hack The Box:** A platform offering a variety of challenges that focus on web application security, reverse engineering, and more.
  - **OverTheWire:** Provides war games that teach security concepts through hands-on practice.

  - **OWASP Juice Shop:** An intentionally vulnerable web application for practicing security testing and secure coding.
- **Secure Coding Workshops:** Conduct workshops where developers can work on secure coding exercises in a guided environment. These workshops should include both theoretical instruction and practical coding sessions.
  Example Workshop Activities:
  - Building and breaking: Developers write code that contains common vulnerabilities and then attempt to exploit them to understand their impact.
  - Refactoring insecure code: Developers are given insecure codebases and tasked with refactoring them to meet secure coding standards.

Integrate Security into the Development Process

- **Adopt Secure Development Lifecycles (SDLC):** Integrate security into every phase of the SDLC, from planning and design through to development, testing, and deployment.
  - **Security in Requirements:** Ensure that security requirements are included in the initial project requirements.
  - **Threat Modeling:** Encourage developers to participate in threat modeling sessions to identify potential security risks early in the design phase.
  - **Security Testing:** Integrate static and dynamic application security testing (SAST and DAST) tools into the CI/CD pipeline to automatically identify vulnerabilities during development.
- **DevSecOps Practices:** Promote the adoption of DevSecOps practices, where security is integrated into the DevOps pipeline. This approach emphasizes collaboration between development, security, and operations teams.
  Key DevSecOps Practices:
  - Automated security testing as part of the CI/CD process
  - Continuous monitoring for security issues in production environments
  - Regular updates to security tools and libraries used in development

Encourage a Security-First Culture

- **Security Champions:** Identify and train security champions within the development teams. These individuals act as advocates for secure coding practices and help bridge the gap between security and development.

Roles of a Security Champion:

- Provide guidance and support to peers on secure coding practices.
- Stay updated on the latest security threats and best practices.
- Lead secure coding initiatives within their teams.

- **Incentives and Recognition:** Provide incentives for developers who consistently demonstrate strong secure coding practices. Recognize and reward developers who contribute to improving the security of the codebase.

  Incentive Programs:
  - Security bounties: Offer rewards for finding and fixing security vulnerabilities within internal projects.
  - Recognition programs: Highlight security-conscious developers in company newsletters, meetings, or through awards.
- **Regular Security Awareness Campaigns:** Conduct regular security awareness campaigns that reinforce the importance of secure coding. Use newsletters, posters, and internal blogs to share tips, best practices, and updates on security trends.

  Campaign Ideas:
  - Monthly secure coding tips sent via email or Slack
  - Security webinars or lunch-and-learn sessions focused on current threats
  - Case studies of past security incidents and how they could have been prevented

Leverage Secure Coding Tools

- **Static Application Security Testing (SAST) Tools:** Use SAST tools to analyze code for security vulnerabilities as it is being written. These tools can automatically detect issues like SQL injection, cross-site scripting, and buffer overflows.

  Examples of SAST Tools:
  - **SonarQube:** An open-source tool that supports multiple languages and provides detailed security analysis.
  - **Checkmarx:** A commercial tool that offers comprehensive static code analysis and integrates with popular development environments.
  - **Fortify Static Code Analyzer:** A widely used tool for identifying security vulnerabilities in source code across multiple languages.
- **Dynamic Application Security Testing (DAST) Tools:** Implement DAST tools to test running applications for vulnerabilities that might not be visible in the source code.

  Examples of DAST Tools:

- **OWASP ZAP:** An open-source tool that helps find security vulnerabilities in web applications.
- **Burp Suite:** A commercial tool widely used for web application security testing, including automated and manual testing capabilities.

- **Interactive Application Security Testing (IAST) Tools:** Use IAST tools to analyze the application during runtime, providing real-time feedback on vulnerabilities as the code is executed.
  Examples of IAST Tools:
  - **Contrast Security:** Provides real-time vulnerability detection as applications are being developed and tested.
  - **Seeker by Synopsys:** Offers detailed insights into how vulnerabilities can be exploited, along with guidance on remediation.
- **Code Quality and Security Linters:** Use linters that enforce secure coding standards and best practices within development environments.
  Examples:
  - **ESLint:** For JavaScript and TypeScript, enforcing secure and consistent coding practices.
  - **Bandit:** For Python, focusing on identifying security issues in code.

Continuous Evaluation and Improvement

- **Regular Assessments:** Conduct regular assessments of the development team's secure coding skills. This can include security-focused code reviews, quizzes, or formal evaluations.
  - **Secure Coding Assessments:** Periodic tests or challenges that assess developers' understanding of secure coding principles.
  - **Metrics:** Track metrics such as the number of vulnerabilities found during code reviews or security scans, and use these metrics to guide further training and improvement.
- **Feedback Loops:** Establish feedback loops where developers receive regular feedback on their code's security, either from automated tools or from security reviews.
  - **Peer Reviews:** Encourage a culture of constructive feedback focused on improving code security during peer reviews.
  - **Security Reports:** Provide detailed security reports from automated tools that highlight vulnerabilities and suggest remediation steps.

- **Update Training Materials:** Regularly update training materials to reflect the latest security threats, vulnerabilities, and best practices. Ensure that training is relevant to the technologies and programming languages used by the development team.
  - **Continuous Curriculum Updates:** Incorporate new security threats and technologies into the training program.
  - **On-Demand Learning:** Provide access to up-to-date training materials and courses that developers can access as needed.

Measuring the Success of Secure Coding Initiatives

To gauge the effectiveness of secure coding initiatives, organizations should establish metrics and track progress over time:

- **Vulnerability Reduction:** Measure the number and severity of vulnerabilities found in code over time. A reduction in vulnerabilities indicates that secure coding practices are being effectively adopted.
- **Code Quality Metrics:** Track code quality metrics that are related to security, such as the number of security issues detected during code reviews or automated scans.
- **Developer Engagement:** Assess developer engagement with secure coding practices through participation in training, code reviews, and security challenges.
- **Incident Response:** Monitor the impact of secure coding practices on incident response times and the number of security incidents attributed to coding errors.

Conclusion

Developing secure coding skills among developers is essential for creating secure, resilient software. By providing comprehensive training, encouraging hands-on practice, integrating security into the development process, and fostering a security-first culture, organizations can empower their developers to write secure code that withstands modern threats. Continuous evaluation and improvement ensure that secure coding practices evolve with the changing threat landscape, ultimately contributing to the overall security and success of the organization's software products.

Continuous Education Through Training and Certifications

Continuous education is a critical component of maintaining and advancing the skills of professionals, especially in fields like information security and software development, where the landscape is constantly evolving. Training and certifications play a vital role in ensuring that individuals stay up-to-date with the latest technologies, threats, best practices, and industry standards. By investing in continuous education, organizations can build a highly skilled workforce capable of addressing emerging challenges and driving innovation.

Importance of Continuous Education

Continuous education offers several key benefits:

- **Keeping Skills Current:** The technology and cybersecurity landscapes evolve rapidly. Continuous education helps professionals stay current with the latest developments, tools, and techniques.
- **Enhancing Job Performance:** Regular training improves job performance by equipping professionals with new skills and knowledge that can be directly applied to their roles.
- **Meeting Compliance Requirements:** Many industries require ongoing training and certifications to meet regulatory and compliance standards, such as ISO 27001, PCI DSS, and GDPR.
- **Career Advancement:** Certifications and advanced training can lead to career growth by demonstrating a commitment to professional development and mastery of specific skills.
- **Improving Organizational Security:** Well-trained employees are better equipped to identify and mitigate security risks, contributing to the overall security posture of the organization.

Types of Continuous Education Opportunities

Continuous education can be pursued through various channels, including formal training programs, certifications, online courses, and hands-on experiences.

Formal Training Programs

- **In-Person Training:** Many organizations offer in-person training sessions, workshops, and boot camps focused on specific skills or technologies. These sessions provide immersive learning experiences with direct interaction between instructors and participants.

Examples of In-Person Training Providers:

- **SANS Institute:** Offers intensive cybersecurity training and certification programs.
- **Global Knowledge:** Provides IT and cybersecurity training, including classroom-based and virtual options.
- **Training Camps:** Short, intensive programs designed to prepare participants for certifications like CISSP, CISM, and CEH.

- **Online Training:** Online platforms offer flexible, self-paced learning opportunities, allowing professionals to study at their own pace and on their schedule. These platforms often provide interactive content, quizzes, and labs.

  Examples of Online Training Platforms:
  - **Coursera:** Offers courses from universities and companies on a wide range of IT and security topics.
  - **Udemy:** Provides a vast catalog of IT and security courses, ranging from beginner to advanced levels.
  - **Pluralsight:** Specializes in technology skills development, offering courses on programming, cloud computing, security, and more.
  - **LinkedIn Learning:** Offers courses on IT, security, and software development, including learning paths for certifications.
- **Custom Training Programs:** Organizations can develop custom training programs tailored to their specific needs, focusing on the technologies, practices, and security requirements most relevant to their environment.

  Benefits of Custom Training:
  - Alignment with organizational goals and technologies
  - Focus on specific skills gaps within the team
  - Opportunity to integrate company-specific policies and practices into the training

Certifications

Certifications are a formal recognition of a professional's expertise in a specific area. They are often required for career advancement and are a valuable way to demonstrate competency in specific skills or knowledge areas.

- **Cybersecurity Certifications:**
  - **CISSP (Certified Information Systems Security Professional):** Recognized globally as a standard of excellence in information security, covering a broad range of security topics.
  - **CEH (Certified Ethical Hacker):** Focuses on the skills needed to identify and exploit vulnerabilities in systems, using the same tools and techniques as malicious hackers.
  - **CISM (Certified Information Security Manager):** Focuses on the management and governance of information security programs.
  - **CompTIA Security+:** An entry-level certification that covers foundational security skills and concepts.
  - **OSCP (Offensive Security Certified Professional):** A hands-on certification focusing on penetration testing and ethical hacking.
- **Software Development Certifications:**
  - **CSSLP (Certified Secure Software Lifecycle Professional):** Focuses on secure software development practices across the entire software development lifecycle (SDLC).
  - **AWS Certified Developer:** Validates proficiency in developing and maintaining applications on the Amazon Web Services platform.
  - **Microsoft Certified: Azure Developer Associate:** Certifies the ability to design, build, test, and maintain cloud applications and services on Microsoft Azure.
  - **Certified Kubernetes Application Developer (CKAD):** Focuses on designing, building, and running applications in Kubernetes.
- **Cloud Certifications:**
  - **AWS Certified Solutions Architect:** Focuses on designing and deploying scalable systems on AWS.
  - **Google Cloud Professional Cloud Architect:** Validates the ability to design, develop, and manage secure, scalable, and reliable cloud architecture.
  - **Microsoft Certified: Azure Solutions Architect Expert:** Certifies the ability to design and implement solutions on Microsoft Azure.
- **Project Management Certifications:**
  - **PMP (Project Management Professional):** Widely recognized as a standard for project management expertise.
  - **PRINCE2 (Projects IN Controlled Environments):** A process-based method for effective project management, widely used in the UK and internationally.

On-the-Job Training and Mentorship

- **Hands-On Projects:** Encourage developers and security professionals to participate in hands-on projects, such as developing new features, implementing security controls, or conducting internal penetration tests. These projects provide practical experience that reinforces learning.
- **Mentorship Programs:** Establish mentorship programs where less experienced employees can learn from senior staff. Mentors can provide guidance on secure coding practices, threat modeling, or how to navigate complex security challenges.
  Benefits of Mentorship:
  - Accelerated learning and skill development
  - Opportunities for real-time feedback and advice
  - Building relationships and knowledge-sharing within the team

Conferences, Webinars, and Workshops

- **Conferences:** Attending industry conferences allows professionals to learn about the latest trends, tools, and best practices in their field. Conferences also provide networking opportunities and exposure to thought leaders.
  Examples of Key Conferences:
  - **Black Hat:** Focuses on the latest in information security research, development, and trends.
  - **RSA Conference:** One of the largest security conferences, covering a broad range of security topics.
  - **DEF CON:** A hacker conference that offers hands-on learning experiences, talks, and competitions.
  - **Google Cloud Next:** Focuses on cloud technology, with sessions on the latest tools, best practices, and innovations.
- **Webinars:** Webinars provide opportunities for continuous learning without the need to travel. They cover a wide range of topics and are often hosted by industry experts.
  Benefits of Webinars:
  - Convenient, accessible from anywhere
  - Interactive Q&A sessions with experts
  - Often free or low-cost
- **Workshops:** Hands-on workshops provide immersive learning experiences, often focusing on specific tools, techniques, or challenges. These can be offered in-person or online and often involve working through real-world scenarios.

Example Workshop Topics:
- Secure DevOps practices
- Implementing zero trust architecture
- Incident response and digital forensics

Online Communities and Forums

- **Discussion Forums:** Participating in online communities and forums such as Stack Overflow, Reddit (e.g., r/netsec, r/cybersecurity), and security-specific forums allows professionals to engage in discussions, share knowledge, and seek advice from peers.
  Benefits:
  - Access to a global community of experts
  - Opportunities to ask questions and share experiences
  - Staying updated on the latest trends and tools
- **Open Source Contributions:** Encourage developers to contribute to open-source projects, especially those focused on security tools and technologies. This provides practical experience and the opportunity to collaborate with a global community of developers.
  Benefits of Open Source Contributions:
  - Real-world coding experience
  - Exposure to industry-standard tools and practices
  - Networking with other professionals in the field

Encouraging Continuous Learning Culture

To maximize the benefits of continuous education, organizations should foster a culture of continuous learning:

Leadership Support

- **Executive Sponsorship:** Ensure that senior leadership supports and prioritizes continuous education. Leaders should advocate for training and certification opportunities, allocate budget, and recognize employees who pursue further education.
- **Align Learning with Business Goals:** Connect continuous education efforts with the organization's strategic goals. For example, if the company is moving to the cloud, encourage certifications in cloud technologies.

Incentives and Recognition

- **Certification Bonuses:** Offer bonuses or other incentives for employees who achieve relevant certifications. This encourages ongoing professional development and recognizes the value of certified skills.

- **Recognition Programs:** Recognize and celebrate employees who complete training programs or earn certifications. Public recognition can be a powerful motivator for continuous learning.
  Examples of Recognition:
  - Acknowledgment in company newsletters or meetings
  - Awarding certificates of achievement
  - Promoting certified employees to roles that leverage their new skills

Continuous Learning Paths

- **Learning Paths:** Create structured learning paths for different roles within the organization, outlining recommended courses, certifications, and training opportunities. Tailor these paths to align with career development goals and organizational needs.
  Example Learning Paths:
  - **For Developers:** Secure coding, DevSecOps, cloud security
  - **For Security Analysts:** Incident response, threat hunting, SOC operations
  - **For IT Managers:** IT governance, compliance, risk management
- **Regular Training Needs Assessment:** Periodically assess the training needs of the organization to ensure that learning opportunities are relevant and aligned with evolving technologies and business requirements.

Continuous Feedback and Improvement

- **Training Effectiveness Surveys:** Gather feedback from employees after they complete training programs to assess the effectiveness and relevance of the content. Use this feedback to continuously improve training offerings.
- **Mentorship and Peer Reviews:** Incorporate regular peer reviews and mentorship into the learning process to reinforce training and provide opportunities for continuous feedback and improvement.

Make Learning Accessible

- **Flexible Learning Options:** Offer a variety of learning formats, such as online courses, in-person workshops, and self-paced modules, to accommodate different learning styles and schedules.

- **On-Demand Resources:** Provide access to on-demand training resources, such as video tutorials, eBooks, and interactive labs, so employees can learn at their own pace and on their schedule.

Measuring the Impact of Continuous Education

To ensure that continuous education efforts are effective, organizations should establish metrics and track progress over time:

- **Certification Attainment:** Track the number of certifications earned by employees and monitor trends over time. This provides insight into the organization's overall skill level and areas of expertise.
- **Skill Development:** Measure improvements in key skills through assessments, performance reviews, and project outcomes. For example, track the reduction in security vulnerabilities in code after secure coding training.
- **Employee Engagement:** Assess employee engagement in continuous education programs by tracking participation rates, course completion rates, and feedback from participants.
- **Business Impact:** Evaluate the impact of continuous education on business outcomes, such as improved security posture, faster incident response times, and increased innovation.

Conclusion

Continuous education through training and certifications is essential for developing and maintaining the skills needed to thrive in today's fast-paced technology and security environments. By providing a variety of learning opportunities, fostering a culture of continuous learning, and supporting employees with incentives and recognition, organizations can ensure that their workforce remains skilled, knowledgeable, and ready to tackle emerging challenges. Regular assessment and improvement of education programs help maintain their relevance and effectiveness, ultimately contributing to the organization's long-term success and security.

Role of Security Champions in Teams

Security champions are individuals within development or IT teams who take on the responsibility of advocating for security best practices, bridging the gap between security teams and developers, and ensuring that security is integrated into the development process. By embedding security expertise within teams, security champions help foster a culture of security, drive secure coding practices, and ensure that security considerations are prioritized throughout the software development lifecycle (SDLC).

Importance of Security Champions

Security champions play a vital role in enhancing an organization's security posture by:

- **Bridging the Security-Development Gap:** Security champions act as a liaison between security teams and development teams, translating security policies into actionable practices and ensuring that security is integrated into daily development activities.
- **Promoting a Security-First Culture:** By advocating for security within their teams, security champions help create a culture where security is seen as everyone's responsibility, not just the domain of the security team.
- **Accelerating Secure Development:** Security champions enable faster adoption of secure development practices by providing on-the-ground guidance and support, which helps developers write more secure code and address vulnerabilities early in the SDLC.
- **Enhancing Communication:** They facilitate better communication between security teams and developers, ensuring that security requirements, risks, and mitigation strategies are clearly understood and implemented.

Key Responsibilities of Security Champions

Security champions have a variety of responsibilities that contribute to the security and resilience of their teams and the broader organization:

Advocate for Secure Coding Practices

- **Promote Best Practices:** Security champions are responsible for promoting secure coding practices within their teams, ensuring that developers are aware of and adhere to security guidelines, such as input validation, secure authentication, and proper error handling.
- **Conduct Code Reviews:** Participate in or lead security-focused code reviews, identifying potential vulnerabilities and guiding developers on how to remediate them.
- **Educate Team Members:** Provide ongoing education and training on secure coding techniques, tools, and emerging threats, helping team members stay informed about the latest security developments.

Serve as a Liaison Between Security and Development Teams

- **Translate Security Requirements:** Security champions help translate high-level security policies and requirements into actionable tasks that developers can implement within their code.
- **Communicate Security Risks:** Ensure that developers understand the security risks associated with their projects, and communicate any concerns or risks identified during development to the security team for further analysis.
- **Facilitate Collaboration:** Act as a point of contact for the security team within the development team, facilitating collaboration and ensuring that security considerations are integrated into the development process from the outset.

Drive Security Awareness and Training

- **Organize Training Sessions:** Coordinate or lead security training sessions, workshops, or lunch-and-learns to raise awareness and improve the security skills of team members.
- **Share Security Updates:** Regularly share updates on new security threats, vulnerabilities, and best practices with the team, ensuring that they are equipped to respond to emerging security challenges.
- **Encourage Participation in Security Activities:** Encourage team members to participate in security activities, such as Capture the Flag (CTF) challenges, security conferences, and online courses, to deepen their security knowledge.

Identify and Mitigate Security Risks

- **Conduct Threat Modeling:** Lead or participate in threat modeling exercises to identify potential security threats during the design and development phases of projects. Help the team understand the potential impact of these threats and how to mitigate them.

- **Integrate Security Tools:** Work with the security team to integrate security tools, such as static and dynamic analysis tools, into the development workflow. Ensure that these tools are used effectively to identify and remediate security issues early in the SDLC.
- **Monitor Security Metrics:** Track security metrics, such as the number of vulnerabilities identified and fixed, to gauge the effectiveness of security practices within the team and identify areas for improvement.

Support Incident Response Efforts

- **Assist in Incident Response:** In the event of a security incident, security champions can assist the incident response team by providing insights into the affected systems, code, and potential vulnerabilities.
- **Conduct Post-Incident Reviews:** Participate in post-incident reviews to analyze the root cause of security incidents, identify lessons learned, and recommend improvements to prevent similar incidents in the future.
- **Improve Resilience:** Use the knowledge gained from incidents to improve the team's overall security posture and resilience against future threats.

Foster a Security-First Culture

- **Lead by Example:** Security champions lead by example, demonstrating a commitment to security in their own work and encouraging others to do the same. They model secure coding practices and prioritize security in all aspects of development.
- **Encourage a Collaborative Approach:** Foster a collaborative environment where security is viewed as a shared responsibility. Encourage open discussions about security concerns and empower team members to raise potential issues.
- **Promote Security as a Business Enabler:** Help the team understand that strong security practices not only protect the organization but also enable the business by building customer trust, ensuring compliance, and preventing costly breaches.

Selecting and Empowering Security Champions

To ensure the success of a security champion program, it's important to carefully select and empower the right individuals:

Selecting Security Champions

- **Technical Expertise:** Security champions should have a strong technical background, with a solid understanding of the development process and secure coding practices. They should be familiar with the technologies and tools used by the development team.
- **Interest in Security:** Look for individuals who have a genuine interest in security and a desire to learn more. Passion for security is a key motivator that drives champions to stay updated on the latest threats and best practices.
- **Leadership and Communication Skills:** Security champions should be effective communicators and capable of leading by example. They need to be able to articulate security concepts clearly and motivate their peers to prioritize security.
- **Problem-Solving Abilities:** Strong problem-solving skills are essential for security champions, as they will need to identify security risks and work with developers to find practical solutions.

Empowering Security Champions

- **Provide Training and Resources:** Equip security champions with the training, resources, and tools they need to succeed. This may include access to security courses, certifications, security tools, and industry conferences.
- **Grant Authority:** Empower security champions with the authority to influence development practices and make decisions related to security within their teams. Ensure that their input is valued and considered in the decision-making process.
- **Encourage Continuous Learning:** Support continuous learning by encouraging security champions to stay updated on the latest security trends and threats. Provide opportunities for them to expand their knowledge and skills.
- **Recognize and Reward Contributions:** Acknowledge the efforts of security champions and reward their contributions to improving the organization's security posture. Public recognition, bonuses, or career advancement opportunities can serve as powerful motivators.

Measuring the Impact of Security Champions

To evaluate the effectiveness of security champions, organizations should track key metrics and outcomes:

- **Reduction in Security Vulnerabilities:** Measure the reduction in security vulnerabilities in the codebase over time, particularly those identified during code reviews or security scans.

- **Increased Security Awareness:** Assess the overall security awareness within the team, as indicated by improved adherence to secure coding practices, participation in security training, and engagement in security-related discussions.
- **Improved Incident Response:** Evaluate the team's ability to respond to and recover from security incidents, noting improvements in incident response times, fewer security-related incidents, and more effective post-incident reviews.
- **Security Metrics:** Track specific security metrics, such as the number of security flaws identified and remediated, the frequency of security-related training, and the level of engagement in security activities.

Challenges and Solutions

While security champions play a crucial role, they may face challenges in their efforts to integrate security into the development process. Here are some common challenges and potential solutions:

- **Challenge: Lack of Time or Resources**
  Solution: Provide dedicated time for security champions to focus on their security responsibilities. Ensure they have access to the necessary tools and resources to perform their duties effectively.

- **Challenge: Resistance to Change**
  Solution: Promote the benefits of secure coding practices and demonstrate how security contributes to overall software quality and business success. Involve security champions in decision-making processes to help them gain buy-in from their peers.

- **Challenge: Keeping Up with Evolving Threats**
  Solution: Encourage continuous learning and provide opportunities for security champions to stay updated on the latest security trends and threats. Support their participation in industry conferences, training sessions, and online courses.

Conclusion

Security champions are instrumental in embedding security into the fabric of development teams. By advocating for secure coding practices, facilitating communication between security and development teams, and fostering a culture of security-first thinking, security champions help ensure that security is prioritized throughout the SDLC. Organizations that empower and support security champions will benefit from stronger security practices, reduced vulnerabilities, and a more resilient security posture overall.

Chapter 10

Security Awareness Programs

Designing Effective Security Awareness Campaigns

Security awareness campaigns are essential for fostering a culture of security within an organization. These campaigns educate employees about the importance of security, inform them about current threats, and provide practical guidance on how to protect the organization's information assets. Effective awareness campaigns can significantly reduce the risk of security incidents caused by human error, such as phishing attacks, weak passwords, or mishandling of sensitive data.

Importance of Security Awareness Campaigns

Security awareness campaigns serve several critical purposes:

- **Reducing Human Error:** A large proportion of security breaches result from human error. Educating employees on security best practices helps mitigate these risks.
- **Promoting a Security-First Culture:** Awareness campaigns reinforce the idea that security is everyone's responsibility, not just the IT or security department's.
- **Ensuring Compliance:** Many regulations and industry standards require organizations to provide regular security awareness training and campaigns to employees.
- **Responding to Emerging Threats:** As new threats emerge, awareness campaigns can quickly educate employees on how to recognize and respond to these threats.

Key Elements of an Effective Security Awareness Campaign

An effective security awareness campaign should be well-planned, engaging, and tailored to the organization's specific needs. The following elements are crucial for success:

Clear Objectives

- **Define Specific Goals:** Start by defining the specific objectives of the campaign. What behaviors are you trying to change? What specific threats are you addressing? For example, you might aim to reduce the number of successful phishing attacks or improve password hygiene across the organization.

- **Measure Success:** Establish metrics to measure the success of the campaign, such as the reduction in phishing click-through rates, the number of reported security incidents, or improvements in security quiz scores.

Targeted Audience Segmentation

- **Segment the Audience:** Tailor the campaign to different groups within the organization, such as executives, IT staff, developers, and general employees. Each group may face different security challenges and require different messaging.
  - **Executives:** Focus on strategic security issues, such as data breaches and compliance.
  - **Developers:** Emphasize secure coding practices and threat modeling.
  - **General Employees:** Address common threats like phishing, social engineering, and secure use of company resources.
- **Role-Specific Training:** Provide role-specific training and content that addresses the unique security challenges faced by different departments or roles within the organization.

Engaging Content and Delivery Methods

- **Use a Variety of Formats:** To keep the audience engaged, use a mix of content formats, such as videos, infographics, quizzes, email tips, webinars, and in-person training sessions.
  - **Videos:** Short, engaging videos can effectively communicate key security concepts and best practices.
  - **Infographics:** Visual content can simplify complex information and make it more memorable.
  - **Quizzes:** Interactive quizzes test employees' knowledge and reinforce learning.
  - **Email Tips:** Regular email tips provide ongoing reminders and updates on security best practices.
- **Storytelling and Real-Life Examples:** Use storytelling and real-life examples to make the content relatable and impactful. Sharing stories of actual security incidents (with anonymized details) can help employees understand the real-world consequences of poor security practices.

Consistent Messaging and Branding

- **Consistent Branding:** Ensure that all campaign materials are consistently branded, using the organization's logos, colors, and design elements. This helps build recognition and reinforces the campaign's message.

- **Reinforce Key Messages:** Identify the core messages you want to convey and repeat them throughout the campaign. Consistent messaging helps ensure that these key points are remembered.

Interactive and Hands-On Learning

- **Simulated Phishing Exercises:** Conduct simulated phishing exercises to test employees' ability to recognize and respond to phishing attempts. Provide immediate feedback and training for those who fall for the simulations.
- **Hands-On Workshops:** Organize workshops that allow employees to practice security skills, such as creating strong passwords, identifying phishing emails, or using multi-factor authentication (MFA).
- **Gamification:** Use gamification techniques, such as leaderboards, badges, or rewards, to make learning more engaging and competitive.

Regular Communication and Reinforcement

- **Ongoing Communication:** Security awareness should not be a one-time event. Regularly communicate security tips, updates, and reminders through various channels, such as email newsletters, intranet posts, or internal chat platforms.
- **Security Awareness Month:** Consider designating a specific month as "Security Awareness Month," during which you can concentrate your efforts on raising awareness and providing intensive training.
- **Pop-Up Reminders:** Use pop-up reminders on company systems to reinforce security best practices, such as reminders to lock screens, use strong passwords, or be cautious with email attachments.

Leadership Involvement

- **Executive Sponsorship:** Secure support from senior leadership to endorse the campaign. When executives publicly advocate for security awareness, it sends a strong message that security is a priority for the entire organization.
- **Visible Participation:** Encourage leaders to participate in the campaign by attending training sessions, sharing their own experiences with security challenges, or sending personalized messages to employees.

Feedback and Continuous Improvement

- **Gather Feedback:** Collect feedback from employees on the effectiveness of the campaign, what they learned, and where they need more guidance. Use surveys, focus groups, or informal conversations to gather insights.
- **Analyze Results:** Review the metrics you established at the beginning of the campaign to assess its impact. Analyze data such as quiz results, phishing simulation outcomes, and incident reports.
- **Iterate and Improve:** Based on the feedback and results, make adjustments to future campaigns. Continuous improvement ensures that each campaign is more effective than the last.

Tools and Resources for Security Awareness Campaigns

There are various tools and resources available to help design, implement, and measure the success of security awareness campaigns:

Security Awareness Platforms

- **KnowBe4:** A comprehensive platform for security awareness training and simulated phishing attacks. It offers a wide range of training content, from videos to interactive modules, and provides detailed reporting on user performance.
- **Cofense PhishMe:** Specializes in phishing awareness training and simulations, helping organizations train employees to recognize and respond to phishing threats.
- **SANS Security Awareness:** Provides security awareness training content, including courses, posters, and newsletters, tailored to different industries and roles.
- **Wombat Security (by Proofpoint):** Offers training modules, assessments, and phishing simulations focused on improving user behavior and reducing security risks.

Communication Tools

- **Intranet Platforms:** Use your organization’s intranet to post regular updates, share training materials, and host interactive content such as quizzes and videos.
- **Email Marketing Tools:** Tools like Mailchimp or Constant Contact can help you design and send engaging email campaigns to employees, complete with tracking and analytics.
- **Learning Management Systems (LMS):** Use an LMS to deliver, track, and manage security awareness training courses. Many LMS

platforms offer features for quizzes, certifications, and progress tracking.

Content Creation Tools

- **Canva:** A user-friendly design tool that allows you to create infographics, posters, and other visual content for your campaign.
- **Powtoon:** A tool for creating animated videos that can explain complex security concepts in a simple and engaging way.
- **Quizlet:** Create custom quizzes to test employees' knowledge on security topics and reinforce learning.

Gamification Tools

- **Kahoot!:** An interactive quiz platform that allows you to create engaging, game-based learning experiences. It's particularly effective for making security training fun and competitive.
- **Badgr:** A tool for creating and awarding digital badges that employees can earn by completing security training modules or challenges.

Measuring the Effectiveness of Security Awareness Campaigns

To ensure that your security awareness campaign is effective, it's important to track and analyze key metrics:

- **Phishing Simulation Results:** Track the number of employees who fall for phishing simulations before and after the campaign. A decrease in click-through rates indicates improved awareness.
- **Quiz and Assessment Scores:** Measure improvement in quiz and assessment scores over time to gauge how well employees are absorbing the information.
- **Incident Reporting:** Monitor the frequency and types of security incidents reported by employees. An increase in reporting may indicate greater awareness and vigilance.
- **Training Completion Rates:** Track the percentage of employees who complete the required training modules. High completion rates suggest strong engagement with the campaign.
- **Behavioral Changes:** Assess changes in employee behavior, such as increased use of strong passwords, better handling of sensitive data, or more frequent use of multi-factor authentication (MFA).

Overcoming Challenges in Security Awareness Campaigns

While security awareness campaigns are critical, they can face several challenges. Here are some common challenges and strategies to overcome them:

- **Challenge: Employee Apathy**
  Solution: Make the content engaging, relevant, and accessible. Use real-life examples, storytelling, and interactive elements to capture attention.

- **Challenge: Lack of Time**
  Solution: Offer training in short, digestible segments that can be completed quickly. Provide on-demand resources so employees can learn at their own pace.

- **Challenge: Keeping Content Up-to-Date**
  Solution: Regularly update training materials to reflect the latest security threats and best practices. Use feedback from employees and incident data to guide updates.

- **Challenge: Measuring Impact**
  Solution: Establish clear metrics at the outset and use tools to track progress. Regularly review and adjust the campaign based on data and feedback.

Conclusion

Designing effective security awareness campaigns is essential for building a strong security culture within an organization. By clearly defining objectives, tailoring content to the audience, using a variety of engaging formats, and continuously reinforcing key messages, organizations can significantly reduce the risk of security incidents caused by human error. Regular measurement and feedback ensure that these campaigns remain relevant and impactful, helping to protect the organization from evolving security threats.

Interactive Learning and Gamified Security Challenges

Interactive learning and gamified security challenges are highly effective methods for engaging employees in security training and reinforcing key security concepts. By making learning experiences interactive and fun, organizations can improve knowledge retention, motivate participation, and foster a deeper understanding of security practices.

Importance of Interactive Learning and Gamification in Security Training

Interactive learning and gamification provide several key benefits:

- **Enhanced Engagement:** Interactive and game-based learning experiences are more engaging than traditional training methods, helping to capture and maintain employees' attention.
- **Improved Knowledge Retention:** Hands-on and experiential learning approaches, such as simulations and games, enhance memory retention by allowing employees to apply concepts in a practical context.
- **Motivation and Competition:** Gamification introduces elements of competition and reward, motivating employees to participate actively and improve their skills.
- **Immediate Feedback:** Interactive learning platforms often provide instant feedback, allowing learners to understand their mistakes and learn from them in real-time.
- **Real-World Application:** Simulated environments and scenarios help employees practice security skills in a safe, controlled setting, preparing them for real-world challenges.

Key Elements of Interactive Learning and Gamified Security Challenges

To design effective interactive learning and gamified security challenges, organizations should consider the following elements:

Realistic Scenarios

- **Simulated Environments:** Create realistic, simulated environments where employees can practice responding to security threats. For example, simulations can mimic phishing attacks, social engineering attempts, or malware infections.

Example Scenarios:

- **Phishing Simulation:** Employees receive simulated phishing emails and are tasked with identifying and reporting them.
- **Incident Response Simulation:** Teams respond to a simulated security breach, identifying the source of the attack, containing the threat, and restoring systems.
- **Secure Coding Challenge:** Developers identify and fix vulnerabilities in a simulated codebase, reinforcing secure coding practices.

- **Hands-On Labs:** Provide hands-on labs where employees can experiment with security tools, configure settings, and troubleshoot issues in a sandboxed environment.

  Example Labs:
  - **Password Cracking Lab:** Employees learn about password security by experimenting with password cracking tools in a controlled environment.
  - **Network Security Lab:** Participants configure firewalls, set up intrusion detection systems (IDS), and monitor network traffic for suspicious activity.

Gamification Elements

- **Points and Scoring:** Assign points for completing challenges, quizzes, or tasks. Points can be awarded based on accuracy, speed, or difficulty level.
  - **Scoring Example:** Employees earn points for correctly identifying phishing emails, with higher points for more sophisticated attacks.
- **Leaderboards:** Display leaderboards to create a sense of competition. Employees can see how they rank compared to their peers, motivating them to improve their performance.
  - **Leaderboard Example:** A company-wide leaderboard shows the top performers in security challenges, with weekly or monthly recognition for high achievers.
- **Badges and Certifications:** Award digital badges or certifications for completing specific challenges or training modules. These can be displayed on the employee's profile or shared on social media.
  - **Badge Example:** Employees earn a "Phishing Pro" badge after successfully completing multiple phishing simulations without falling for any traps.
- **Levels and Progression:** Implement levels or progression paths where employees can advance by completing increasingly complex challenges. This helps maintain engagement over time.

    - **Progression Example:** Employees start with basic security challenges and advance to more complex scenarios as they demonstrate proficiency.

Interactive Quizzes and Assessments

- **Interactive Quizzes:** Use interactive quizzes to reinforce learning and assess employees' understanding of security concepts. Quizzes can include multiple-choice questions, true/false statements, or scenario-based questions.
    - **Quiz Example:** After completing a training module on password security, employees take a quiz to test their knowledge, with immediate feedback on their answers.
- **Scenario-Based Assessments:** Present employees with realistic scenarios and ask them to choose the best course of action. This helps evaluate their decision-making skills in real-world situations.
    - **Scenario Example:** Employees are presented with a scenario where they receive an unexpected email from a colleague asking for sensitive information. They must decide whether to respond, report the email, or take another action.

Collaborative Team Challenges

- **Team-Based Competitions:** Organize team-based security challenges where groups of employees work together to solve problems, identify vulnerabilities, or respond to simulated incidents. Collaboration encourages knowledge sharing and teamwork.
    - **Team Challenge Example:** Teams compete in a Capture the Flag (CTF) challenge, where they solve security puzzles and identify vulnerabilities to earn points for their team.
- **Escape Room Scenarios:** Create virtual or physical escape room challenges with a security theme, where teams must solve puzzles and complete tasks to "escape" from a simulated threat.
    - **Escape Room Example:** Teams are "trapped" in a virtual environment where they must solve a series of security-related puzzles, such as decrypting messages or finding hidden vulnerabilities, to escape.

Ongoing Learning and Challenges

- **Monthly Challenges:** Introduce monthly security challenges that focus on different topics, such as phishing, secure coding, or data protection. This keeps security awareness top of mind throughout the year.

    - **Challenge Example:** A monthly phishing challenge where employees are tested with new phishing simulations and can earn points for correctly identifying threats.
- **Security Awareness Games:** Develop or use existing security awareness games that employees can play during breaks or as part of training sessions. These games can reinforce key concepts in a fun and engaging way.
    - **Game Example:** A game where employees must defend a virtual network from attackers by implementing security controls and responding to threats.

Reward and Recognition

- **Incentives for Participation:** Offer rewards, such as gift cards, extra time off, or other perks, for employees who actively participate in gamified challenges and achieve high scores.
    - **Incentive Example:** Employees who reach a certain level in a security training program receive a voucher for a lunch or coffee break.
- **Recognition Programs:** Publicly recognize top performers in security challenges through company newsletters, team meetings, or award ceremonies. Recognition can be a powerful motivator.
    - **Recognition Example:** A quarterly award for the "Top Security Champion" based on performance in security challenges and contributions to team security efforts.

Tools and Platforms for Interactive Learning and Gamified Challenges

There are various tools and platforms available to facilitate interactive learning and gamified security challenges:

Capture the Flag (CTF) Platforms

- **Hack The Box:** An online platform that offers a variety of CTF challenges focused on penetration testing, ethical hacking, and cybersecurity.
- **CTFd:** An open-source CTF platform that allows organizations to create and manage their own CTF challenges, including custom scenarios and scoring systems.
- **TryHackMe:** A gamified platform that provides hands-on security challenges in a virtual environment, suitable for both beginners and experienced professionals.

Security Awareness and Gamification Platforms

- **KnowBe4:** A platform that offers security awareness training with gamification features, such as leaderboards, badges, and simulated phishing tests.
- **CyberHoot:** Provides security awareness training with interactive learning modules and quizzes, as well as gamified elements like badges and progress tracking.
- **Wombat Security (by Proofpoint):** Offers security awareness training with interactive modules, quizzes, and phishing simulations that include gamified features.

Learning Management Systems (LMS) with Gamification Features

- **Moodle:** An open-source LMS that can be customized with gamification plugins to include points, badges, and leaderboards in security training courses.
- **TalentLMS:** An LMS that includes built-in gamification features, such as badges, points, and leaderboards, to enhance engagement in training programs.
- **Docebo:** A cloud-based LMS that offers gamification options, including challenges, rewards, and social learning features, to make security training more interactive.

Interactive Quiz and Game Creation Tools

- **Kahoot!:** A popular tool for creating interactive quizzes and games that can be used in training sessions, meetings, or as part of ongoing security awareness programs.
- **Quizlet:** Allows the creation of custom quizzes and flashcards that can be used for interactive learning and gamified training.
- **EdApp:** A microlearning platform with gamification features, including quizzes, leaderboards, and real-time feedback, designed to make learning more engaging.

Measuring the Effectiveness of Interactive Learning and Gamified Challenges

To assess the impact of interactive learning and gamified security challenges, organizations should track key metrics and outcomes:

- **Participation Rates:** Monitor the number of employees participating in interactive learning activities and gamified challenges. High participation rates indicate strong engagement.

- **Knowledge Retention:** Evaluate improvements in knowledge retention through pre- and post-training assessments or quizzes. Compare scores to measure learning gains.
- **Behavioral Changes:** Track changes in employee behavior, such as increased reporting of phishing emails, improved password practices, or better adherence to security policies.
- **Performance Improvement:** Measure improvements in performance, such as reduced click-through rates on phishing simulations, faster incident response times, or more secure coding practices.
- **Feedback and Satisfaction:** Gather feedback from participants to assess their satisfaction with the interactive learning experience and identify areas for improvement.

Challenges and Solutions in Implementing Interactive Learning and Gamified Challenges

While interactive learning and gamification are powerful tools, they can present challenges. Here are some common challenges and strategies to overcome them:

- **Challenge: Resource Constraints**
  Solution: Start small with existing gamified platforms or free tools, and gradually expand as resources allow. Consider partnering with external vendors or using open-source solutions.

- **Challenge: Employee Resistance**
  Solution: Clearly communicate the benefits of participating in interactive learning and gamified challenges. Highlight how these activities contribute to both personal and organizational security.

- **Challenge: Maintaining Engagement Over Time**
  Solution: Introduce new challenges and content regularly to keep the experience fresh and engaging. Offer rewards and recognition to sustain motivation.

- **Challenge: Measuring Impact**
  Solution: Establish clear metrics at the outset and use tools to track participation, performance, and behavioral changes. Regularly review and adjust the program based on data and feedback.

Conclusion

Interactive learning and gamified security challenges are highly effective methods for engaging employees in security training and reinforcing key concepts. By creating realistic scenarios, incorporating gamification elements, and offering hands-on experiences, organizations can significantly improve knowledge retention, motivate participation, and enhance overall security awareness. Regular measurement and continuous improvement ensure that these training initiatives remain effective and relevant, ultimately contributing to a stronger security culture and reduced risk of security incidents.

Measuring the Impact of Awareness Programs

Measuring the impact of security awareness programs is crucial for understanding their effectiveness and making data-driven decisions to enhance their reach and impact. Effective measurement provides insights into how well the program is changing behavior, improving security practices, and reducing risk within the organization.

Importance of Measuring Awareness Program Impact

Understanding the impact of security awareness programs is important for several reasons:

- **Demonstrating Value:** Provides evidence of the program's effectiveness, helping to justify the investment in security training and awareness initiatives.
- **Identifying Gaps:** Helps identify areas where the program may be falling short, allowing for targeted improvements.
- **Driving Continuous Improvement:** Regular measurement and analysis support ongoing refinement and optimization of the awareness program.
- **Supporting Compliance:** Many regulations and standards require organizations to assess the effectiveness of their security awareness efforts.

Key Metrics for Measuring Awareness Program Impact

To effectively measure the impact of a security awareness program, organizations should track a variety of metrics that cover different aspects of behavior change, knowledge retention, and risk reduction.

Participation and Engagement Metrics

- **Training Completion Rates:** Measure the percentage of employees who complete the required training modules. High completion rates indicate strong engagement with the program.
  - **Example:** Track the number of employees who have completed phishing awareness training within a specified timeframe.
- **Participation in Interactive Activities:** Monitor participation in interactive activities, such as quizzes, simulations, or gamified

challenges. This can indicate how actively employees are engaging with the material.

  - **Example:** Count the number of employees who participated in a simulated phishing exercise or a security escape room challenge.

- **Attendance at Live Events:** Track attendance at live training sessions, webinars, or workshops. High attendance rates suggest that employees value and prioritize security training.
  - **Example:** Record the number of employees who attended a security awareness webinar on data protection.

Knowledge Retention and Improvement Metrics

- **Pre- and Post-Training Assessments:** Use assessments to measure knowledge before and after training. Improvements in scores indicate that employees are learning and retaining key security concepts.
  - **Example:** Compare pre-training quiz scores with post-training scores to measure knowledge gains in areas like password security or phishing awareness.
- **Quiz and Test Scores:** Track the scores on quizzes or tests taken after completing training modules. High or improving scores suggest that employees are grasping the material.
  - **Example:** Analyze the average score on a phishing identification quiz to gauge understanding of phishing threats.
- **Survey Feedback:** Collect feedback through surveys to assess employees' perceptions of their own security knowledge and confidence. Surveys can also capture suggestions for improving the program.
  - **Example:** Use a survey to ask employees how confident they feel in identifying phishing emails after training.

Behavioral Change Metrics

- **Phishing Simulation Results:** Measure the outcomes of phishing simulations, such as the click-through rate on simulated phishing emails. A reduction in click-through rates over time indicates improved awareness and caution.
  - **Example:** Track the percentage of employees who clicked on a simulated phishing email before and after the awareness program was implemented.
- **Incident Reporting Rates:** Monitor the number of security incidents reported by employees, such as suspected phishing attempts or unauthorized access. An increase in reporting may indicate greater vigilance and awareness.

- **Example:** Compare the number of phishing incidents reported by employees before and after targeted phishing training.

- **Secure Behavior Adoption:** Track the adoption of secure behaviors, such as the use of strong passwords, multi-factor authentication (MFA), and data encryption. This can be measured through system logs, password audits, or security tool usage metrics.
  - **Example:** Measure the percentage of employees who have enabled MFA on their accounts after an MFA awareness campaign.

Risk Reduction and Security Posture Metrics

- **Reduction in Security Incidents:** Measure the reduction in the number or severity of security incidents attributed to human error. Fewer incidents suggest that employees are applying what they've learned from the awareness program.
  - **Example:** Track the number of successful phishing attacks or data breaches over time.
- **Time to Detect and Respond:** Monitor the time it takes for employees to detect and report security threats. Faster detection and response times indicate a more vigilant and responsive workforce.
  - **Example:** Measure the average time it takes for employees to report a phishing email after receiving it.
- **Vulnerability Remediation Rates:** Track the speed and effectiveness of remediation efforts following the identification of security vulnerabilities. Improved remediation rates suggest that the awareness program is influencing faster and more effective responses.
  - **Example:** Compare the average time taken to patch vulnerabilities in employee workstations before and after a vulnerability management training.

Program Satisfaction and Feedback Metrics

- **Employee Satisfaction:** Assess employee satisfaction with the awareness program through surveys or feedback forms. High satisfaction levels indicate that the program is well-received and likely to be effective.
  - **Example:** Use a post-training survey to ask employees how satisfied they are with the quality and relevance of the training content.
- **Program Improvement Suggestions:** Collect suggestions from employees on how to improve the awareness program. This feedback can provide valuable insights into areas where the program could be more effective or engaging.

    - **Example:** Include an open-ended question in a survey asking employees for their suggestions on making security training more interactive.

Compliance and Audit Metrics

- **Compliance with Training Requirements:** Track compliance with mandatory training requirements, especially in regulated industries. Ensure that all employees complete required training within specified timelines.
    - **Example:** Monitor the percentage of employees who have completed GDPR compliance training.
- **Audit Results:** Evaluate the results of internal or external audits related to security awareness and training. Positive audit outcomes indicate that the program is meeting compliance standards.
    - **Example:** Review audit findings related to employee security training and awareness practices.

Tools and Techniques for Measuring Awareness Program Impact

Organizations can use various tools and techniques to collect and analyze the metrics associated with security awareness programs:

Learning Management Systems (LMS)

- **Tracking Completion and Scores:** Use an LMS to track training completion rates, quiz scores, and assessment results. Many LMS platforms also offer reporting features that allow you to analyze performance data.
    - **Examples of LMS:** TalentLMS, Moodle, Docebo

Phishing Simulation Platforms

- **Monitoring Phishing Results:** Platforms like KnowBe4, PhishMe (by Cofense), and Wombat Security (by Proofpoint) offer phishing simulation tools that track metrics such as click-through rates, reporting rates, and susceptibility trends.
    - **Features:** Automated phishing campaigns, real-time reporting, detailed analytics

Survey Tools

- **Collecting Feedback:** Use survey tools like SurveyMonkey, Google Forms, or Microsoft Forms to gather feedback from employees on the effectiveness of the training and their confidence in applying what they've learned.

- **Features:** Customizable surveys, real-time results, analysis tools

Security Information and Event Management (SIEM) Systems

- **Monitoring Behavior and Incidents:** SIEM systems like Splunk, IBM QRadar, or LogRhythm can track security incidents, employee behavior (e.g., logins, MFA usage), and response times. This data can be correlated with training efforts to measure impact.
  - **Features:** Real-time monitoring, incident correlation, advanced analytics

HR and Performance Management Systems

- **Tracking Compliance:** Use HR systems to track compliance with training requirements and integrate performance metrics related to security behavior into employee evaluations.
  - **Examples of Systems:** Workday, BambooHR, SAP SuccessFactors

Feedback Loops and Continuous Improvement

- **Regular Review Meetings:** Hold regular review meetings with key stakeholders (e.g., HR, IT, security) to discuss the results of the awareness program, identify areas for improvement, and plan future initiatives.
  - **Agenda Items:** Review of metrics, employee feedback, discussion of new threats, planning for upcoming training

Continuous Improvement Based on Measurement

Measuring the impact of a security awareness program is not a one-time activity; it should be part of a continuous improvement process:

Analyze and Interpret Data

- **Identify Trends:** Look for trends in the data that indicate areas of improvement or ongoing challenges. For example, if phishing simulation click-through rates are decreasing, this suggests improved awareness, but consistent incidents may indicate a need for further training.
- **Benchmarking:** Compare your organization's performance against industry benchmarks to see how your awareness program stacks up.

Adjust the Program Based on Insights

- **Targeted Interventions:** Use the insights gained from measurements to design targeted interventions. For example, if you notice that a particular department is struggling with phishing awareness, consider providing additional, focused training.

- **Content Updates:** Regularly update the training content based on new threats, employee feedback, and performance data to keep it relevant and engaging.
- **Iterative Improvements:** Implement changes incrementally and monitor their impact, making further adjustments as needed to refine the program.

Communicate Results and Successes

- **Report to Stakeholders:** Regularly communicate the results of the awareness program to stakeholders, including senior management. Highlight successes, such as improved metrics or reduced incidents, to demonstrate the program's value.
- **Celebrate Milestones:** Celebrate key milestones, such as reaching a certain percentage of training completion or achieving a significant reduction in security incidents. This can help reinforce the importance of the program and maintain momentum.

Conclusion

Measuring the impact of security awareness programs is essential for understanding their effectiveness, driving continuous improvement, and demonstrating their value to the organization. By tracking key metrics related to participation, knowledge retention, behavioral change, risk reduction, and employee satisfaction, organizations can ensure that their awareness programs are achieving their goals and contributing to a stronger security posture. Regular analysis and adjustments based on measurement results help keep the program relevant, engaging, and effective in mitigating security risks.

Chapter 11

Communication and Collaboration

Best Practices for Cross-Functional Communication in Security

Effective cross-functional communication is crucial for ensuring that security is integrated into all aspects of an organization's operations. Security is not just the responsibility of the IT or security teams; it involves collaboration across departments, including HR, legal, compliance, operations, and development teams. By fostering clear and consistent communication between these groups, organizations can improve their security posture, ensure compliance, and mitigate risks more effectively.

Importance of Cross-Functional Communication in Security

Cross-functional communication is vital for several reasons:

- **Holistic Security Approach:** Security risks often span multiple departments, requiring input and action from various teams. Effective communication ensures that all relevant stakeholders are aware of security issues and can contribute to their resolution.
- **Timely Incident Response:** Clear communication channels enable quick and coordinated responses to security incidents, reducing the impact on the organization.
- **Alignment with Business Goals:** Security initiatives need to align with broader business objectives. Cross-functional communication helps ensure that security strategies support and enable the organization's goals.
- **Compliance and Risk Management:** Ensuring that all departments understand and comply with security policies and regulations is crucial for managing risk and avoiding penalties.

Best Practices for Cross-Functional Communication in Security

To enhance cross-functional communication in security, organizations should implement the following best practices:

Establish Clear Communication Channels

- **Designated Points of Contact:** Assign designated points of contact (POCs) in each department who are responsible for security-related communications. These POCs should be well-versed in the security needs of their respective departments and be able to relay information effectively.

    - **Example:** Appoint a security liaison in HR to handle communications related to employee data protection and insider threats.

- **Communication Platforms:** Use centralized communication platforms that allow for easy sharing of security information, such as collaboration tools (e.g., Microsoft Teams, Slack) or secure email channels. Ensure that these platforms are accessible to all relevant stakeholders.
    - **Example:** Create a dedicated security channel in Slack where updates, alerts, and discussions can take place.

Regular Cross-Functional Meetings

- **Security Committees:** Establish a cross-functional security committee that includes representatives from key departments. This committee should meet regularly to discuss security issues, review incidents, and coordinate on security initiatives.
    - **Example:** Hold monthly security committee meetings with representatives from IT, HR, legal, and compliance to review ongoing security projects and address new threats.
- **Incident Response Meetings:** During security incidents, convene cross-functional incident response meetings to ensure that all relevant teams are aligned and can coordinate their actions effectively.
    - **Example:** In the event of a data breach, bring together IT, legal, PR, and compliance teams to discuss the response strategy and ensure that all aspects of the incident are being addressed.

Clear and Consistent Messaging

- **Standardized Terminology:** Use standardized terminology when discussing security topics to avoid confusion and ensure that all departments understand the issues at hand. Provide a glossary of common security terms if needed.
    - **Example:** Define key terms like "phishing," "data breach," and "encryption" in a shared document accessible to all teams.
- **Tailored Communication:** Tailor security messages to the specific needs and concerns of each department. Avoid overly technical language when communicating with non-technical teams, and focus on the implications for their work.

    - **Example:** When discussing a new security policy with HR, emphasize how it affects employee data management and the steps HR needs to take to comply.

Shared Goals and Metrics

- **Align Security with Business Objectives:** Ensure that security goals are aligned with the overall business objectives of the organization. Communicate how security initiatives support these goals, such as protecting customer data or ensuring regulatory compliance.
    - **Example:** Demonstrate to the marketing team how securing customer data enhances brand trust and supports customer retention efforts.
- **Common Metrics:** Establish common security metrics that are meaningful to all departments and use these metrics to track progress and report on the success of security initiatives.
    - **Example:** Track metrics such as the number of phishing incidents reported, time to patch vulnerabilities, and compliance with security training requirements.

Promote a Security-First Culture

- **Top-Down Support:** Ensure that senior leadership actively supports and participates in cross-functional security communication. Leadership's commitment to security sets the tone for the entire organization.
    - **Example:** Have the CEO or CIO regularly communicate the importance of security in all-hands meetings or company newsletters.
- **Security Champions:** Identify and empower security champions within each department who can advocate for security best practices, relay important information, and act as a resource for their colleagues.
    - **Example:** A security champion in the development team might lead secure coding practices and ensure that security is considered throughout the software development lifecycle (SDLC).

Continuous Education and Awareness

- **Ongoing Training:** Provide continuous security training that is relevant to each department's role. This training should emphasize the importance of cross-functional communication and collaboration in maintaining security.

- **Example:** Offer tailored training sessions for legal teams on data protection regulations and for HR teams on secure employee onboarding and offboarding processes.
- **Awareness Campaigns:** Run regular security awareness campaigns that emphasize the importance of cross-functional collaboration in achieving security goals.
  - **Example:** A campaign might focus on the shared responsibility of protecting sensitive information, highlighting how each department plays a role in securing the organization.

Feedback Loops and Continuous Improvement

- **Gather Feedback:** Regularly solicit feedback from all departments on the effectiveness of security communications and the overall security strategy. Use this feedback to make improvements.
  - **Example:** Conduct surveys or hold focus groups with department representatives to gather insights on how security communication can be improved.
- **Iterate and Adapt:** Continuously refine communication strategies based on feedback, changes in the threat landscape, and evolving business needs. Be open to adapting communication methods as necessary.
  - **Example:** If a department finds the current communication tools ineffective, explore alternative platforms or formats that better suit their needs.

Documentation and Knowledge Sharing

- **Centralized Documentation:** Maintain a centralized repository of security policies, procedures, and guidelines that is accessible to all departments. Ensure that this documentation is kept up-to-date and easily navigable.
  - **Example:** Use a platform like Confluence or SharePoint to store and organize security documentation, making it searchable and accessible to all employees.
- **Knowledge Sharing Sessions:** Host regular knowledge-sharing sessions where different departments can present on security-related topics or share lessons learned from incidents.
  - **Example:** After a security incident, the IT team might share their experience and lessons learned with other departments to help prevent similar issues in the future.

Overcoming Challenges in Cross-Functional Security Communication

While cross-functional communication is essential, it can also present challenges. Here are some common challenges and strategies to overcome them:

Siloed Departments

- **Challenge:** Departments may operate in silos, with limited communication and collaboration on security issues.
- **Solution:** Break down silos by establishing regular cross-functional meetings, creating shared goals, and encouraging interdepartmental collaboration on security initiatives.

Varying Levels of Security Knowledge

- **Challenge:** Different departments may have varying levels of security knowledge, leading to misunderstandings or miscommunication.
- **Solution:** Provide tailored training and resources to bring all departments up to a baseline level of security knowledge. Use clear, jargon-free language when communicating complex security concepts.

Resistance to Change

- **Challenge:** Some departments may resist adopting new security practices or changing existing workflows.
- **Solution:** Communicate the benefits of security initiatives in terms of how they support business goals and protect the organization. Involve resistant departments in the decision-making process to gain buy-in.

Information Overload

- **Challenge:** Employees may feel overwhelmed by the volume of security information and alerts.
- **Solution:** Prioritize and filter information to ensure that employees receive relevant, actionable security communications. Avoid overloading them with unnecessary details.

Tools and Technologies for Cross-Functional Communication

Organizations can leverage various tools and technologies to facilitate effective cross-functional communication in security:

Collaboration Platforms

- **Microsoft Teams:** A collaboration platform that allows for real-time communication, file sharing, and integration with other tools. Create dedicated security channels for cross-functional teams.
- **Slack:** A messaging platform that supports team communication, file sharing, and integration with security tools. Use Slack to create dedicated channels for incident response and security updates.

Project Management Tools

- **Jira:** A project management tool that can be used to track security-related tasks, incidents, and projects. Jira's integration with other tools makes it useful for coordinating cross-functional security efforts.
- **Trello:** A simple project management tool that can be used to manage security initiatives and track progress on cross-functional tasks.

Knowledge Management Systems

- **Confluence:** A knowledge management tool that allows teams to document and share security policies, procedures, and best practices. Use Confluence to create a centralized repository for security documentation.
- **SharePoint:** A collaboration and document management platform that can be used to store and organize security-related documents and resources.

Security Information and Event Management (SIEM) Systems

- **Splunk:** A SIEM platform that provides real-time monitoring, analysis, and alerting on security events. Use Splunk to share security data across departments and coordinate responses.
- **IBM QRadar:** Another SIEM solution that helps teams analyze security incidents and coordinate responses across different departments.

Incident Response Platforms

- **TheHive:** An open-source incident response platform that facilitates communication and coordination among cross-functional teams during security incidents.
- **Cortex XSOAR:** A Security Orchestration, Automation, and Response (SOAR) platform that integrates with various security tools and facilitates cross-functional incident response efforts.

Conclusion

Effective cross-functional communication is essential for building a strong security posture across the entire organization. By establishing clear communication channels, fostering collaboration, aligning security goals with business objectives, and leveraging appropriate tools, organizations can ensure that all departments work together to address security challenges. Continuous education, feedback loops, and a shared commitment to security help create a culture where security is everyone's responsibility, ultimately leading to a more resilient organization.

Integrating Security into DevSecOps

Integrating security into DevSecOps is essential for building secure, resilient software while maintaining the agility and speed of modern development practices. DevSecOps extends the principles of DevOps—collaboration, automation, and continuous delivery—by embedding security into every phase of the software development lifecycle (SDLC). This approach ensures that security is not an afterthought but a fundamental part of the development process.

Importance of Integrating Security into DevSecOps

Integrating security into DevSecOps offers several key benefits:

- **Shift-Left Security:** By addressing security earlier in the development process, organizations can identify and fix vulnerabilities before they reach production, reducing the risk of security breaches.
- **Faster Incident Response:** DevSecOps enables continuous monitoring and quick responses to security incidents, minimizing potential damage.
- **Automation of Security Tasks:** Automating security testing and compliance checks allows teams to maintain speed and efficiency while ensuring that security standards are met.
- **Collaboration Across Teams:** DevSecOps fosters collaboration between development, security, and operations teams, ensuring that security considerations are aligned with business goals.

Key Practices for Integrating Security into DevSecOps

To effectively integrate security into DevSecOps, organizations should adopt the following practices:

Shift-Left Security Testing

- **Early Security Testing:** Integrate security testing early in the SDLC, during the coding and build stages, to identify and address vulnerabilities before they propagate through the development pipeline.
  - **Example:** Implement static application security testing (SAST) tools to analyze code for vulnerabilities as developers write it.

- **Continuous Security Testing:** Implement security testing at every stage of the development pipeline, including unit tests, integration tests, and deployment stages.
  - **Example:** Use dynamic application security testing (DAST) tools to test running applications for security vulnerabilities during the integration and testing phases.

Automate Security Processes

- **Security as Code:** Treat security policies, configurations, and compliance checks as code, integrating them into the CI/CD pipeline. This allows security checks to be automated and consistently applied across all environments.
  - **Example:** Use infrastructure as code (IaC) tools like Terraform or AWS CloudFormation to automate the deployment of secure infrastructure, including network configurations, access controls, and encryption settings.
- **Automated Security Scans:** Integrate automated security scanning tools into the CI/CD pipeline to continuously monitor for vulnerabilities and ensure compliance with security standards.
  - **Example:** Automate vulnerability scans using tools like OWASP ZAP, SonarQube, or Nessus as part of the build process.

Implement Continuous Monitoring

- **Real-Time Security Monitoring:** Implement continuous security monitoring to detect threats, anomalies, and vulnerabilities in real-time. This involves monitoring applications, networks, and infrastructure for security events.
  - **Example:** Use a Security Information and Event Management (SIEM) system like Splunk or IBM QRadar to aggregate and analyze security events from across the DevOps pipeline.
- **Log Management:** Centralize log management to monitor application and system logs for security-relevant events, such as unauthorized access attempts or suspicious activity.
  - **Example:** Implement log aggregation tools like ELK Stack (Elasticsearch, Logstash, Kibana) or Fluentd to collect and analyze logs from various sources in the pipeline.

Foster Collaboration Between Development, Security, and Operations Teams

- **Cross-Functional Teams:** Create cross-functional teams that include members from development, security, and operations. This ensures that security considerations are integrated throughout the entire development process.

  - **Example:** Establish regular meetings where development, security, and operations teams review security requirements, discuss potential risks, and collaborate on solutions.

- **Security Champions:** Identify and empower security champions within development teams to advocate for secure coding practices and ensure that security is prioritized during development.
  - **Example:** Security champions participate in code reviews, threat modeling sessions, and security testing, serving as a bridge between the security and development teams.

Embed Security into CI/CD Pipelines

- **Secure CI/CD Pipelines:** Secure the CI/CD pipeline itself by implementing security controls, such as access management, code signing, and secret management. This ensures that the pipeline cannot be compromised or used to introduce vulnerabilities into the software.
  - **Example:** Use tools like HashiCorp Vault to securely manage and store secrets (e.g., API keys, passwords) used in the CI/CD pipeline.
- **Automated Compliance Checks:** Integrate automated compliance checks into the CI/CD pipeline to ensure that code meets security and regulatory requirements before it is deployed to production.
  - **Example:** Automate compliance checks using tools like Chef InSpec or OpenSCAP to verify that configurations and deployments adhere to security policies.

Conduct Regular Threat Modeling and Risk Assessments

- **Threat Modeling:** Perform threat modeling exercises early in the development process to identify potential security threats and design mitigations. Threat modeling helps teams understand the security risks associated with their applications and make informed design decisions.
  - **Example:** Use tools like Microsoft Threat Modeling Tool or OWASP Threat Dragon to facilitate threat modeling sessions with development teams.
- **Risk Assessments:** Conduct regular risk assessments to evaluate the security risks associated with new features, changes, or technologies. This helps prioritize security efforts and allocate resources effectively.
  - **Example:** Develop a risk assessment framework that includes evaluating the impact and likelihood of potential security threats and using this assessment to guide security decisions.

Continuous Security Education and Awareness

- **Ongoing Security Training:** Provide continuous security training for developers, operations, and security teams to keep them updated on the latest security threats, best practices, and tools.
  - **Example:** Offer regular training sessions on secure coding practices, DevSecOps principles, and the use of security tools integrated into the CI/CD pipeline.
- **Security Awareness Campaigns:** Run security awareness campaigns that emphasize the importance of security in DevOps practices and encourage teams to adopt a security-first mindset.
  - **Example:** Launch a campaign highlighting common security risks in DevOps, such as misconfigured cloud resources or unpatched vulnerabilities, and provide tips for mitigating these risks.

Secure Development Environments

- **Isolated Development Environments:** Ensure that development environments are isolated from production environments to prevent unauthorized access and minimize the risk of security breaches.
  - **Example:** Use containerization tools like Docker to create isolated, reproducible development environments that mirror production settings.
- **Endpoint Security:** Implement endpoint security measures on all devices used in the development process to protect against malware, unauthorized access, and data loss.
  - **Example:** Deploy endpoint detection and response (EDR) solutions on developer workstations to monitor and protect against threats.

Tools and Technologies for Integrating Security into DevSecOps

To successfully integrate security into DevSecOps, organizations can leverage various tools and technologies:

Security Testing Tools

- **Static Application Security Testing (SAST):**
  - **SonarQube:** A tool that analyzes source code for security vulnerabilities, code quality, and compliance with coding standards.
  - **Checkmarx:** A SAST solution that scans code for security issues and provides developers with detailed remediation guidance.

- **Dynamic Application Security Testing (DAST):**
  - **OWASP ZAP:** An open-source DAST tool that helps identify security vulnerabilities in running applications.
  - **Burp Suite:** A comprehensive web vulnerability scanner used to find and exploit security weaknesses in web applications.
- **Software Composition Analysis (SCA):**
  - **WhiteSource:** A tool that scans open-source components in the software to detect vulnerabilities, license risks, and outdated libraries.
  - **Snyk:** A developer-friendly tool that helps find and fix vulnerabilities in open-source dependencies and container images.

Continuous Integration and Continuous Deployment (CI/CD) Tools

- **Jenkins:** An open-source automation server that facilitates the continuous integration and delivery of software. Jenkins can be integrated with security tools to automate security testing in the pipeline.
- **GitLab CI:** A CI/CD platform that integrates security testing, code quality checks, and compliance verification into the development pipeline.

Security Monitoring and Incident Response Tools

- **Splunk:** A SIEM platform that provides real-time security monitoring, log analysis, and incident response capabilities.
- **ELK Stack (Elasticsearch, Logstash, Kibana):** A log management and analysis toolset that helps monitor security events and detect anomalies in real-time.

Infrastructure as Code (IaC) Tools

- **Terraform:** An IaC tool that allows teams to define and manage infrastructure using code, ensuring that security configurations are consistently applied across environments.
- **AWS CloudFormation:** A service that helps automate the deployment of AWS resources, including security controls, through IaC templates.

Secret Management Tools

- **HashiCorp Vault:** A tool for securely storing and managing sensitive information such as API keys, passwords, and certificates used in the DevOps pipeline.

- **AWS Secrets Manager:** A service that helps manage and rotate secrets used in AWS environments, ensuring that sensitive data is protected throughout the CI/CD process.

Measuring the Success of DevSecOps Integration

To evaluate the effectiveness of integrating security into DevSecOps, organizations should track key metrics and outcomes:

- **Vulnerability Detection Rates:** Measure the number of vulnerabilities detected during different stages of the SDLC. A higher detection rate in earlier stages indicates successful shift-left security practices.
- **Time to Remediate:** Track the time it takes to remediate security issues once they are identified. Faster remediation times suggest that security is well-integrated into the development process.
- **Compliance with Security Policies:** Monitor compliance with security policies and standards, such as code quality, encryption, and access controls, across the CI/CD pipeline.
- **Incident Response Times:** Measure the speed and effectiveness of incident response efforts, including detection, containment, and remediation.
- **Security Training Participation:** Track participation rates in security training programs and the adoption of secure coding practices among developers.

Overcoming Challenges in Integrating Security into DevSecOps

While integrating security into DevSecOps is essential, it can also present challenges. Here are some common challenges and strategies to overcome them:

Balancing Security and Speed

- **Challenge:** DevOps teams may be concerned that integrating security will slow down the development process.
- **Solution:** Focus on automating security tasks to minimize disruption and maintain development speed. Prioritize high-impact security measures that can be implemented without significant delays.

Lack of Security Expertise

- **Challenge:** Development teams may lack the security expertise needed to effectively implement DevSecOps practices.

- **Solution:** Provide ongoing security training and resources to upskill developers. Consider embedding security experts or champions within development teams to provide guidance and support.

Resistance to Change
- **Challenge:** Teams may resist adopting new security practices, especially if they perceive them as adding complexity or overhead.
- **Solution:** Communicate the benefits of DevSecOps, such as reduced security risks and improved compliance. Involve teams in the decision-making process to gain buy-in and address concerns.

Tool Integration Challenges
- **Challenge:** Integrating security tools into existing CI/CD pipelines can be complex and time-consuming.
- **Solution:** Start with small, incremental integrations and gradually expand the scope of security automation. Choose tools that easily integrate with existing DevOps platforms and workflows.

Conclusion

Integrating security into DevSecOps is essential for building secure, resilient software that meets the demands of modern development practices. By adopting shift-left security testing, automating security processes, fostering collaboration between development, security, and operations teams, and continuously monitoring security throughout the SDLC, organizations can ensure that security is an integral part of their DevOps practices. Overcoming challenges and leveraging the right tools and techniques will enable organizations to achieve a successful DevSecOps transformation, ultimately leading to a stronger security posture and reduced risk of security incidents.

Managing Third-Party Relationships and Security Expectations

In today's interconnected business environment, organizations often rely on third-party vendors, partners, and service providers to support their operations. While these relationships can bring significant benefits, they also introduce additional security risks. Managing third-party relationships effectively involves ensuring that these external entities adhere to your organization's security policies, standards, and expectations to protect sensitive data and maintain compliance with regulatory requirements.

Importance of Managing Third-Party Security

Managing third-party security is crucial for several reasons:

- **Data Protection:** Third parties often have access to sensitive data, making it essential to ensure that they handle and protect this data in line with your security standards.
- **Regulatory Compliance:** Many regulations, such as GDPR, HIPAA, and PCI DSS, require organizations to manage the security practices of their third-party providers.
- **Risk Mitigation:** Third-party breaches can have severe consequences, including financial losses, reputational damage, and legal liabilities. Effective management of third-party security reduces the risk of such incidents.
- **Business Continuity:** Ensuring that third-party providers have robust security practices helps maintain business continuity by minimizing the likelihood of disruptions due to security incidents.

Key Practices for Managing Third-Party Relationships and Security Expectations

To effectively manage third-party relationships and ensure security expectations are met, organizations should adopt the following practices:

Conduct Thorough Due Diligence

- **Vendor Assessment:** Before engaging with a third party, conduct a thorough assessment of their security practices. This may include reviewing their security policies, certifications, and compliance with relevant regulations.

    - **Example:** Use a vendor security questionnaire to gather information about the third party's security controls, data protection practices, and incident response capabilities.
- **Risk Assessment:** Perform a risk assessment to identify potential security risks associated with the third party. Consider factors such as the type of data they will access, the services they will provide, and their history of security incidents.
    - **Example:** Assess the third party's risk profile based on factors like the sensitivity of the data they handle, their geographic location, and their industry sector.

Establish Clear Security Requirements

- **Contractual Security Clauses:** Include specific security requirements in contracts with third parties. These clauses should outline the security controls that the third party must implement, as well as their responsibilities for data protection and incident response.
    - **Example:** Include clauses that require the third party to implement encryption for sensitive data, maintain up-to-date security patches, and undergo regular security audits.
- **Service Level Agreements (SLAs):** Define security-related SLAs that specify performance metrics, response times, and penalties for non-compliance with security requirements.
    - **Example:** An SLA might require the third party to notify your organization within 24 hours of a security breach and to remediate vulnerabilities within a specified timeframe.

Monitor and Audit Third-Party Security

- **Regular Security Audits:** Conduct regular security audits of third-party providers to ensure they are meeting your security requirements. Audits can be performed by internal teams or independent third-party assessors.
    - **Example:** Schedule annual security audits that include on-site visits, review of security documentation, and testing of security controls.
- **Continuous Monitoring:** Implement continuous monitoring of third-party security practices, such as monitoring their compliance with SLAs, vulnerability management, and incident response activities.
    - **Example:** Use tools to monitor third-party network traffic, access logs, and security events to detect any unusual activity or potential security breaches.

Foster Ongoing Communication and Collaboration

- **Regular Communication:** Maintain regular communication with third-party providers to discuss security issues, share updates on threats, and coordinate on incident response efforts.
  - **Example:** Hold quarterly security review meetings with key third-party providers to discuss security performance, upcoming changes, and areas for improvement.
- **Incident Reporting:** Establish clear communication channels for reporting security incidents. Ensure that third parties are aware of their responsibilities to report incidents promptly and cooperate with your organization during the response.
  - **Example:** Define a standard incident reporting process that third parties must follow, including the types of incidents that must be reported and the timeframe for doing so.

Implement a Third-Party Risk Management Program

- **Risk Management Framework:** Develop a comprehensive third-party risk management program that includes policies, procedures, and tools for assessing and managing the security risks associated with third-party relationships.
  - **Example:** Use a risk management framework like NIST or ISO 27001 to structure your third-party risk management program and ensure it aligns with best practices.
- **Vendor Risk Tiers:** Categorize third-party providers into risk tiers based on the level of access they have to sensitive data and systems. Apply different levels of scrutiny and oversight depending on the risk tier.
  - **Example:** Assign high-risk vendors, such as those handling sensitive customer data, to a higher risk tier that requires more frequent audits and tighter security controls.

Provide Security Awareness and Training

- **Third-Party Training:** Provide security awareness training to third-party providers to ensure they understand your security expectations and are equipped to meet them.
  - **Example:** Offer online training modules that cover topics like data protection, secure data handling, and incident response for third-party staff who interact with your systems or data.
- **Shared Best Practices:** Share security best practices and resources with third parties to help them improve their security posture and align with your organization's standards.

- **Example:** Distribute a security best practices guide to third-party vendors, outlining key principles for securing data and systems.

Plan for Incident Response and Business Continuity

- **Incident Response Coordination:** Ensure that third parties are integrated into your organization's incident response plan. This includes defining roles, responsibilities, and communication protocols in the event of a security incident.
  - **Example:** Conduct joint incident response drills with key third-party providers to test coordination and communication during a simulated security breach.
- **Business Continuity Planning:** Verify that third parties have their own business continuity and disaster recovery plans in place, and ensure these plans are aligned with your organization's requirements.
  - **Example:** Review third-party business continuity plans to ensure they address potential disruptions to services that are critical to your organization.

Review and Update Third-Party Relationships Regularly

- **Ongoing Risk Reviews:** Conduct regular reviews of third-party relationships to assess whether they continue to meet your security requirements and align with your risk management strategy.
  - **Example:** Perform annual reviews of all third-party providers to assess their security performance and determine whether any changes are needed in the relationship.
- **Termination Clauses:** Include termination clauses in contracts that allow your organization to end the relationship if the third party fails to meet security expectations or poses an unacceptable risk.
  - **Example:** A contract might include a clause that allows for termination if the third party experiences a significant data breach or fails to remediate critical vulnerabilities within a reasonable timeframe.

Tools and Technologies for Managing Third-Party Security

Organizations can leverage various tools and technologies to manage third-party security effectively:

Vendor Risk Management Platforms

- **Prevalent:** A platform that automates third-party risk assessments, manages vendor relationships, and provides continuous monitoring of vendor security performance.

- **BitSight:** A security ratings platform that provides real-time data on the security posture of third-party vendors, allowing organizations to assess and monitor vendor risk.
- **ProcessUnity:** A risk management platform that offers tools for assessing, managing, and monitoring third-party risks across the vendor lifecycle.

Security Assessment Tools

- **SecurityScorecard:** A tool that provides security ratings and continuous monitoring of third-party vendors based on publicly available data, allowing organizations to assess vendor risk.
- **Qualys:** A security platform that offers vulnerability assessments, compliance checks, and continuous monitoring of third-party networks and systems.

Compliance Management Tools

- **OneTrust:** A platform that helps organizations manage third-party compliance with privacy regulations, data protection laws, and security standards.
- **RSA Archer:** A governance, risk, and compliance (GRC) platform that provides tools for managing third-party risk, assessing vendor compliance, and tracking regulatory obligations.

Contract Management Tools

- **DocuSign:** A digital contract management tool that facilitates the creation, signing, and management of contracts with third-party vendors, including security clauses and SLAs.
- **Concord:** A contract lifecycle management platform that helps organizations manage vendor contracts, track compliance with security requirements, and automate contract renewals.

Incident Response Platforms

- **TheHive:** An incident response platform that supports coordination and communication between your organization and third-party vendors during security incidents.
- **Cortex XSOAR:** A Security Orchestration, Automation, and Response (SOAR) platform that integrates with third-party systems to automate incident response processes and enhance collaboration.

Measuring the Effectiveness of Third-Party Security Management

To assess the effectiveness of your third-party security management efforts, organizations should track key metrics and outcomes:

- **Vendor Compliance Rates:** Measure the percentage of third-party vendors that meet your security requirements and comply with contractual obligations.
  - **Example:** Track the number of vendors that have completed required security assessments and implemented recommended security controls.
- **Incident Response Times:** Monitor the time it takes for third-party vendors to report security incidents and their effectiveness in responding to and resolving issues.
  - **Example:** Measure the average time taken by vendors to notify your organization of a security breach and the time required to remediate vulnerabilities.
- **Audit Results:** Track the results of security audits conducted on third-party vendors, including the number of findings, the severity of issues, and the time taken to address them.
  - **Example:** Review audit reports to identify common security gaps among vendors and areas where additional oversight may be needed.
- **Risk Reduction:** Evaluate the overall reduction in third-party security risks based on risk assessments, monitoring results, and incident data.
  - **Example:** Track the reduction in high-risk vendors or the decrease in security incidents related to third-party providers over time.

Overcoming Challenges in Managing Third-Party Security

Managing third-party security can present challenges. Here are some common challenges and strategies to overcome them:

Limited Visibility into Third-Party Practices

- **Challenge:** Organizations may have limited visibility into the security practices of third-party vendors, making it difficult to assess and monitor their security posture.
- **Solution:** Use continuous monitoring tools and require regular security assessments and audits to gain better visibility into third-party practices.

Resistance from Third-Party Vendors

- **Challenge:** Third-party vendors may resist implementing additional security controls or undergoing regular audits, citing cost or resource constraints.
- **Solution:** Clearly communicate the importance of security requirements, include them in contracts, and offer support or resources to help vendors meet expectations.

Managing a Large Number of Vendors

- **Challenge:** Organizations with a large number of third-party vendors may struggle to manage security assessments, monitoring, and compliance across all relationships.
- **Solution:** Implement a vendor risk management platform to automate assessments, categorize vendors by risk level, and prioritize oversight for high-risk vendors.

Keeping Up with Regulatory Changes

- **Challenge:** Keeping up with changing regulatory requirements and ensuring that third-party vendors remain compliant can be challenging.
- **Solution:** Use compliance management tools to track regulatory changes and ensure that contracts and security requirements are updated accordingly.

Conclusion

Managing third-party relationships and security expectations is critical for protecting sensitive data, maintaining regulatory compliance, and mitigating risks associated with external partners. By conducting thorough due diligence, establishing clear security requirements, monitoring vendor performance, and fostering ongoing communication and collaboration, organizations can effectively manage third-party security. Leveraging appropriate tools and technologies, measuring the effectiveness of security management efforts, and addressing challenges proactively will help organizations build strong, secure partnerships with their third-party vendors.

Part 6
Conclusion

The Evolving Nature of Threats and the Need for Continuous Adaptation

The digital landscape is in a constant state of flux, with new threats emerging regularly as technology advances. Cybercriminals are increasingly sophisticated, leveraging cutting-edge tools and tactics to exploit vulnerabilities in systems, applications, and networks. In this environment, organizations cannot afford to be complacent. Continuous adaptation to evolving threats is essential to maintaining a robust security posture and protecting sensitive data and assets.

Understanding the Evolving Nature of Cyber Threats

Cyber threats evolve rapidly due to several factors:

- **Technological Advancements:** As new technologies such as cloud computing, artificial intelligence (AI), and the Internet of Things (IoT) become more widespread, they introduce new attack surfaces and vulnerabilities that cybercriminals can exploit.
- **Sophisticated Attack Techniques:** Cybercriminals continuously develop more sophisticated attack techniques, including advanced persistent threats (APTs), ransomware, and zero-day exploits. These techniques often bypass traditional security measures.
- **Automation of Attacks:** The use of automated tools and malware-as-a-service (MaaS) platforms allows cybercriminals to launch large-scale attacks with minimal effort, increasing the frequency and impact of cyber incidents.
- **Globalization of Threat Actors:** Cyber threats are no longer confined to specific regions; they are global. Threat actors include nation-states, organized crime groups, hacktivists, and insider threats, each with different motivations and capabilities.
- **Regulatory Changes:** Evolving regulatory requirements, such as GDPR, CCPA, and others, necessitate continuous adaptation to ensure compliance and avoid penalties.

The Need for Continuous Adaptation

To effectively combat evolving cyber threats, organizations must embrace continuous adaptation in their security strategies:

Continuous Threat Monitoring and Intelligence

- **Real-Time Threat Monitoring:** Implement real-time threat monitoring to detect and respond to emerging threats as they occur. This involves using Security Information and Event Management (SIEM) systems, endpoint detection and response (EDR) tools, and other monitoring solutions.
  - **Example:** Deploy a SIEM system that aggregates and analyzes security events from across the organization's network, identifying anomalies that may indicate a cyber attack.
- **Threat Intelligence Integration:** Incorporate threat intelligence feeds into security operations to stay informed about the latest threats, vulnerabilities, and attack methods. This information can help organizations anticipate and prepare for new threats.
  - **Example:** Subscribe to threat intelligence services that provide updates on new malware strains, phishing campaigns, and vulnerabilities targeting specific industries.

Agile Security Practices

- **Agile Security Framework:** Adopt an agile security framework that allows for rapid adaptation to new threats. This involves iterative security assessments, frequent updates to security controls, and continuous improvement based on feedback and new information.
  - **Example:** Implement a DevSecOps approach that integrates security into every phase of the development lifecycle, allowing for quick identification and mitigation of vulnerabilities as new code is developed.
- **Risk-Based Security:** Prioritize security efforts based on risk assessments that consider the likelihood and impact of various threats. This approach ensures that resources are focused on the most significant risks.
  - **Example:** Conduct regular risk assessments to identify high-risk areas, such as critical infrastructure or sensitive data repositories, and prioritize the implementation of security controls in these areas.

Adaptive Defense Mechanisms

- **Adaptive Security Architecture:** Develop a security architecture that can adapt to changing threats. This includes implementing technologies such as artificial intelligence (AI) and machine learning (ML) that can analyze patterns, detect anomalies, and respond to threats in real-time.

- **Example:** Use ML-based anomaly detection tools that learn normal user behavior and automatically detect deviations that may indicate a security breach.

- **Layered Security:** Implement a layered security approach, also known as defense in depth, where multiple security measures are used to protect against different types of threats. This ensures that if one layer is breached, others remain in place to provide protection.
  - **Example:** Combine firewalls, intrusion detection systems (IDS), antivirus software, encryption, and user access controls to create a comprehensive defense against cyber attacks.

Continuous Security Education and Training

- **Ongoing Training Programs:** Provide continuous security training to employees to keep them informed about the latest threats and best practices. Regular training helps ensure that employees remain vigilant and aware of new attack methods.
  - **Example:** Offer monthly security awareness sessions that cover topics such as phishing, social engineering, and secure data handling, with updates on emerging threats.
- **Phishing Simulations and Drills:** Conduct regular phishing simulations and incident response drills to test employees' ability to recognize and respond to threats. These exercises help reinforce training and identify areas for improvement.
  - **Example:** Send simulated phishing emails to employees to assess their ability to detect and report phishing attempts, followed by targeted training for those who fall for the simulation.

Regular Review and Update of Security Policies

- **Dynamic Policy Management:** Regularly review and update security policies to reflect changes in the threat landscape, technological advancements, and regulatory requirements. Policies should be flexible enough to adapt to new challenges without compromising security.
  - **Example:** Review the organization's data protection policy annually to ensure it aligns with the latest regulatory requirements and best practices for data security.
- **Incident Response Plan Updates:** Continuously update the incident response plan (IRP) based on lessons learned from past incidents, new threat intelligence, and changes in the organization's infrastructure or operations.

  - **Example:** After a security incident, conduct a post-incident review to identify weaknesses in the IRP and make necessary updates to improve response capabilities.

Collaborative Security Efforts

- **Cross-Industry Collaboration:** Participate in cross-industry collaboration and information-sharing initiatives, such as ISACs (Information Sharing and Analysis Centers) or cybersecurity working groups. Sharing information about threats and best practices with peers can help organizations stay ahead of emerging threats.
  - **Example:** Join an industry-specific ISAC to receive and share threat intelligence with other organizations in the same sector, enhancing collective security efforts.
- **Public-Private Partnerships:** Engage in public-private partnerships to collaborate on cybersecurity initiatives, share resources, and access government-provided threat intelligence and support.
  - **Example:** Partner with government agencies or cybersecurity organizations to receive early warnings about threats targeting critical infrastructure and access to resources for incident response.

Tools and Technologies for Continuous Adaptation

Organizations can leverage a variety of tools and technologies to support continuous adaptation to evolving threats:

Security Information and Event Management (SIEM) Systems

- **Splunk:** A SIEM platform that provides real-time monitoring, correlation, and analysis of security events, enabling rapid detection and response to threats.
- **IBM QRadar:** Another SIEM solution that helps organizations detect, prioritize, and respond to security incidents by analyzing log data, network traffic, and user activity.

Threat Intelligence Platforms

- **Recorded Future:** A threat intelligence platform that aggregates data from multiple sources to provide actionable insights on emerging threats and vulnerabilities.
- **ThreatConnect:** A platform that integrates threat intelligence with security operations, allowing organizations to make informed decisions based on the latest threat data.

Endpoint Detection and Response (EDR) Tools

- **CrowdStrike Falcon:** An EDR solution that provides advanced threat detection and response capabilities, using AI to identify and mitigate threats in real-time.
- **Carbon Black:** A cloud-based EDR platform that continuously monitors endpoints for suspicious activity and enables rapid response to potential threats.

Anomaly Detection and Behavioral Analysis

- **Darktrace:** An AI-driven platform that uses machine learning to detect anomalies and potential threats by analyzing patterns of behavior across the network.
- **Vectra AI:** A platform that applies behavioral analysis and AI to detect, investigate, and respond to threats in real-time.

Security Awareness and Training Platforms

- **KnowBe4:** A security awareness training platform that offers simulated phishing tests, interactive training modules, and tools for measuring employee vulnerability to social engineering attacks.
- **Cofense:** A platform that provides phishing simulation and training solutions, helping organizations build resilience against phishing attacks.

Measuring the Effectiveness of Continuous Adaptation

To assess the effectiveness of continuous adaptation to evolving threats, organizations should track key metrics and outcomes:

- **Threat Detection Rates:** Monitor the percentage of threats detected early in the attack lifecycle. An increase in early detection rates indicates improved adaptability to new threats.
  - **Example:** Track the number of zero-day vulnerabilities detected and mitigated before exploitation.
- **Response Times:** Measure the time it takes to respond to and contain security incidents. Faster response times suggest that the organization is effectively adapting to evolving threats.
  - **Example:** Compare the average time to detect and remediate incidents before and after implementing new monitoring tools or updating the incident response plan.
- **Training Effectiveness:** Evaluate the effectiveness of security training programs by tracking employee performance in phishing simulations and incident response drills.

  - **Example:** Monitor the reduction in the percentage of employees who fall for phishing simulations over time.
- **Policy Compliance:** Assess compliance with updated security policies and procedures, ensuring that employees and systems are aligned with the latest security standards.
  - **Example:** Track the completion rate of required security training and adherence to updated security policies across the organization.

Overcoming Challenges in Continuous Adaptation

Continuous adaptation to evolving threats can present challenges. Here are some common challenges and strategies to overcome them:

Resource Constraints

- **Challenge:** Adapting to evolving threats requires continuous investment in tools, training, and personnel, which can strain resources.
- **Solution:** Prioritize security investments based on risk assessments, focusing on high-impact areas. Leverage automation and AI-driven tools to maximize efficiency and reduce the burden on security teams.

Keeping Up with Rapid Changes

- **Challenge:** The pace of change in the threat landscape can make it difficult to stay current with the latest threats and best practices.
- **Solution:** Invest in threat intelligence services and continuous learning programs to ensure that the organization remains informed and prepared to adapt to new threats.

Resistance to Change

- **Challenge:** Employees and teams may resist changes to security policies or procedures, especially if they perceive them as disruptive.
- **Solution:** Communicate the importance of adaptability in maintaining security and involve employees in the process of updating and implementing new security measures.

Conclusion

The evolving nature of cyber threats necessitates continuous adaptation in an organization's security strategies and practices. By implementing real-time threat monitoring, adopting agile security frameworks, leveraging adaptive defense mechanisms, providing ongoing security training, and fostering collaboration across industries, organizations can effectively combat new and emerging threats. Continuous adaptation is not a one-time effort but an ongoing process that requires vigilance, flexibility, and a commitment to staying ahead of the threat landscape.

The Future of Information Security in Software Development

As technology continues to evolve at a rapid pace, the field of information security in software development is also undergoing significant changes. The future of information security in software development will be shaped by emerging technologies, evolving threat landscapes, and increasing regulatory demands. To stay ahead, organizations must adapt to these changes and integrate cutting-edge security practices into their development processes.

Key Trends Shaping the Future of Information Security in Software Development

Several key trends are expected to influence the future of information security in software development:

Rise of Artificial Intelligence and Machine Learning

- **AI-Powered Security:** Artificial Intelligence (AI) and Machine Learning (ML) will play a critical role in enhancing information security by automating threat detection, analysis, and response. These technologies can analyze vast amounts of data to identify patterns and anomalies that may indicate security threats, enabling faster and more accurate responses.
  - **Example:** AI-driven security tools that automatically detect and mitigate zero-day vulnerabilities by analyzing code patterns and predicting potential attack vectors.
- **Adversarial AI:** As AI becomes more prevalent in security, attackers will also begin using AI to develop more sophisticated attacks. This will lead to an ongoing battle between defensive and offensive AI systems.
  - **Example:** AI-powered malware that can adapt and evolve to evade detection by traditional security measures, requiring new defense strategies.

Increasing Adoption of DevSecOps

- **Security as Code:** The shift towards DevSecOps—integrating security into the entire software development lifecycle—will continue to gain momentum. Security practices will be embedded into development pipelines, making security a shared responsibility among developers, security teams, and operations.

  - **Example:** Automated security testing tools integrated into CI/CD pipelines, allowing for continuous security assessments throughout the development process.

- **Collaboration and Automation:** DevSecOps will emphasize collaboration between cross-functional teams and the automation of security tasks to ensure that security is not a bottleneck but an enabler of rapid development.
  - **Example:** Automated compliance checks that verify adherence to security policies and standards before code is deployed to production.

The Proliferation of Cloud-Native Applications

- **Cloud Security Challenges:** As more organizations move to cloud-native architectures, securing these environments will become increasingly complex. Security will need to address the unique challenges of multi-cloud environments, containerization, and microservices.
  - **Example:** Implementing security controls that protect data and applications across multiple cloud platforms while ensuring consistent security policies.
- **Zero Trust Architecture:** The adoption of Zero Trust security models will become more widespread, particularly in cloud environments. This approach assumes that threats exist both inside and outside the network, requiring continuous verification of every user, device, and application.
  - **Example:** Enforcing granular access controls, multi-factor authentication, and continuous monitoring to secure cloud-native applications and services.

Evolution of Threats and Attack Vectors

- **Sophisticated Cyber Threats:** Cyber threats will continue to evolve, with attackers using more advanced techniques such as AI-driven attacks, supply chain compromises, and targeted ransomware campaigns. Security strategies will need to evolve to counter these threats.
  - **Example:** Enhanced threat intelligence platforms that provide real-time insights into emerging threats and help organizations proactively defend against sophisticated attacks.

- **Supply Chain Security:** As software development increasingly relies on third-party components and open-source libraries, securing the software supply chain will become a top priority. Organizations will need to ensure that all components, including dependencies, are free from vulnerabilities.
  - **Example:** Implementing software composition analysis (SCA) tools that continuously monitor and assess the security of third-party libraries used in applications.

Regulatory and Compliance Demands

- **Stricter Regulations:** Governments and regulatory bodies will impose stricter security and privacy regulations, especially in industries handling sensitive data such as healthcare, finance, and critical infrastructure. Compliance will require robust security practices throughout the software development lifecycle.
  - **Example:** Compliance with regulations such as GDPR, CCPA, and the forthcoming regulations for AI and IoT, which will mandate stricter data protection and security measures.
- **Continuous Compliance:** The concept of continuous compliance will gain traction, where organizations continuously monitor and audit their security posture to ensure ongoing compliance with regulatory requirements.
  - **Example:** Continuous compliance platforms that automatically track and report on an organization's adherence to various regulatory standards in real-time.

Increased Focus on Privacy-By-Design

- **Privacy-By-Design Principles:** Privacy-by-design will become a fundamental aspect of software development, with privacy considerations being integrated from the very beginning of the development process. This approach ensures that data protection is a core feature of all applications.
  - **Example:** Implementing privacy-enhancing technologies (PETs) such as differential privacy, data anonymization, and encryption by default in software applications.
- **Data Minimization:** Developers will increasingly adopt data minimization practices, collecting only the data necessary for the intended purpose and ensuring that it is stored and processed securely.
  - **Example:** Designing applications that limit the collection and retention of personal data, reducing the potential impact of data breaches.

Preparing for the Future of Information Security in Software Development

Organizations must take proactive steps to prepare for the future of information security in software development:

Embrace Continuous Learning and Innovation

- **Ongoing Education:** Ensure that developers, security teams, and other stakeholders are continuously educated on the latest security trends, tools, and best practices. This includes staying informed about emerging threats and regulatory changes.
  - **Example:** Regularly update training programs to include new security frameworks, coding practices, and threat intelligence.
- **Encourage Innovation:** Foster a culture of innovation where security teams are encouraged to experiment with new technologies and approaches to improve security. This might involve adopting AI-driven security tools, exploring blockchain for secure transactions, or integrating quantum-resistant encryption algorithms.
  - **Example:** Establish innovation labs or security hackathons where teams can test and implement cutting-edge security solutions in a controlled environment.

Invest in Advanced Security Technologies

- **AI and Machine Learning:** Invest in AI and ML technologies to enhance threat detection, automate security processes, and predict potential vulnerabilities in code.
  - **Example:** Deploy AI-driven tools that analyze code repositories for vulnerabilities, identify potential exploits, and suggest remediations before code is deployed.
- **Quantum-Resistant Security:** As quantum computing becomes more of a reality, start exploring quantum-resistant encryption methods to protect sensitive data from future quantum attacks.
  - **Example:** Begin researching and testing post-quantum cryptography algorithms to future-proof encryption practices against quantum computing threats.

Strengthen Collaboration Across Teams

- **Cross-Functional Collaboration:** Foster stronger collaboration between development, security, and operations teams through

DevSecOps practices. Ensure that security is a shared responsibility and that all teams work together to address security challenges.
  - **Example:** Implement regular cross-functional meetings, collaborative threat modeling sessions, and integrated workflows that involve security at every stage of development.
- **Security Champions:** Develop a network of security champions within development teams who can advocate for secure coding practices, lead security initiatives, and serve as liaisons with the security team.
  - **Example:** Train and empower developers to become security champions who can drive security improvements within their teams and promote a security-first mindset.

Focus on Secure Software Supply Chain Management

- **Supply Chain Security Measures:** Implement robust security measures to protect the software supply chain, including the use of trusted sources for third-party components, continuous monitoring of dependencies, and regular audits of supplier security practices.
  - **Example:** Adopt software bill of materials (SBOM) practices to track and manage all components and dependencies used in software projects, ensuring transparency and security throughout the supply chain.
- **Collaborate with Suppliers:** Work closely with third-party vendors and suppliers to ensure they adhere to your organization's security standards and practices.
  - **Example:** Establish formal agreements with suppliers that include security requirements, regular assessments, and incident response protocols.

Adopt a Zero Trust Security Model

- **Zero Trust Principles:** Adopt a Zero Trust security model that assumes no entity—whether inside or outside the network—can be trusted by default. Implement continuous verification of identities, devices, and access privileges.
  - **Example:** Use identity and access management (IAM) solutions that enforce multi-factor authentication, least privilege access, and real-time monitoring of user behavior.
- **Micro-Segmentation:** Implement micro-segmentation to create isolated segments within the network, limiting the ability of attackers to move laterally if they gain access.

    - **Example:** Segment critical systems and data into isolated environments that require separate authentication and authorization, reducing the risk of widespread compromise.

Prioritize Privacy and Ethical Considerations

- **Ethical AI and Privacy:** As AI and data-driven technologies become more prevalent, prioritize ethical considerations in the development and deployment of software. This includes ensuring transparency, fairness, and accountability in AI systems and protecting user privacy.
    - **Example:** Implement ethical AI guidelines that ensure AI-driven applications do not discriminate, violate privacy, or operate without transparency.
- **Data Protection by Design:** Incorporate data protection principles into the design and architecture of software applications, ensuring that privacy and security are foundational aspects of the development process.
    - **Example:** Design applications with built-in data encryption, access controls, and privacy-enhancing technologies from the outset.

The Role of Leadership in Shaping the Future of Information Security

Leadership will play a critical role in driving the future of information security in software development:

Visionary Leadership

- **Setting the Vision:** Leaders must set a clear vision for integrating security into software development, emphasizing its importance as a strategic priority and aligning security goals with broader business objectives.
    - **Example:** A CTO might establish a company-wide initiative to embed security into every stage of the SDLC, with measurable goals and outcomes.
- **Inspiring Innovation:** Encourage a culture of innovation where security is seen as an enabler of business growth and competitive advantage, rather than a hindrance.
    - **Example:** Leadership might sponsor research into emerging security technologies, such as AI-driven security or quantum cryptography, and support their integration into development practices.

Strategic Investment

- **Allocating Resources:** Leaders must allocate the necessary resources—budget, talent, and technology—to support advanced security initiatives and ensure the organization is prepared for future challenges.
  - **Example:** Investing in a state-of-the-art security operations center (SOC) equipped with the latest threat detection and response technologies.
- **Talent Development:** Focus on attracting, retaining, and developing top talent in security, AI, and software development to stay ahead of the curve in security innovation.
  - **Example:** Offering competitive salaries, continuous learning opportunities, and career advancement paths for security professionals and developers.

Building a Security-First Culture

- **Promoting a Security-First Mindset:** Leaders must champion a security-first mindset across the organization, ensuring that security is ingrained in the culture and values of the company.
  - **Example:** Implementing security awareness programs that reach all employees, from executives to developers, emphasizing the role everyone plays in maintaining security.
- **Accountability and Transparency:** Foster accountability and transparency in security practices, ensuring that security decisions are made collaboratively and that the organization is open about its security efforts.
  - **Example:** Regularly reporting on the organization's security posture to stakeholders, including board members, employees, and customers.

Conclusion

The future of information security in software development will be shaped by technological advancements, evolving threats, and changing regulatory landscapes. Organizations that embrace continuous innovation, integrate security into every aspect of their development processes, and prioritize collaboration across teams will be well-positioned to navigate these challenges. By investing in advanced security technologies, adopting forward-thinking security models like DevSecOps and Zero Trust, and fostering a security-first culture, organizations can build resilient, secure software that meets the demands of the future. Leadership will play a pivotal role in driving this transformation, ensuring that security is not just a technical requirement but a strategic advantage in the ever-changing digital landscape.

Final Thoughts on Maintaining a Robust ISMS

Maintaining a robust Information Security Management System (ISMS) is crucial for any organization seeking to protect its information assets, ensure compliance with regulatory requirements, and build trust with customers and stakeholders. A well-implemented ISMS provides a structured approach to managing information security risks, aligning security efforts with business objectives, and fostering a culture of continuous improvement. Here are some final thoughts on maintaining a strong and effective ISMS:

Commitment from Leadership

- **Leadership Support:** The success of an ISMS depends heavily on the commitment and support of senior leadership. Leaders must champion information security as a strategic priority, allocate the necessary resources, and ensure that security objectives are aligned with the organization's overall goals.
- **Setting the Tone:** Leadership should set the tone for a security-first culture by actively participating in security initiatives, communicating the importance of security to all employees, and holding everyone accountable for their role in maintaining security.

Continuous Risk Management

- **Proactive Risk Assessment:** Regularly assess and identify risks to the organization's information assets. This involves not only evaluating existing risks but also anticipating emerging threats and vulnerabilities as the business environment and technology landscape evolve.
- **Dynamic Risk Treatment:** Implement and continuously update risk treatment plans to address identified risks. This includes applying appropriate security controls, monitoring their effectiveness, and adjusting strategies as needed to mitigate new or changing risks.

Integration of Security into Business Processes

- **Security by Design:** Ensure that security is integrated into all business processes and operations from the outset. This includes embedding security into the software development lifecycle, supply chain management, and day-to-day business activities.

- **Alignment with Business Objectives:** The ISMS should align with the organization's business objectives, ensuring that security efforts support and enhance overall business performance rather than hinder it.

Continuous Improvement and Adaptation

- **Regular Audits and Reviews:** Conduct regular internal and external audits of the ISMS to ensure compliance with standards such as ISO 27001 and to identify areas for improvement. Audits should be seen as opportunities to refine and strengthen the ISMS.
- **Learning from Incidents:** Treat security incidents as learning opportunities. After every incident, conduct a thorough post-incident review to identify root causes, assess the effectiveness of the response, and implement improvements to prevent recurrence.
- **Adaptation to Change:** The ISMS should be flexible and adaptable to changes in the regulatory environment, technological advancements, and evolving business needs. Regularly review and update policies, procedures, and controls to keep pace with these changes.

Employee Engagement and Awareness

- **Ongoing Training and Awareness:** Continuously educate and train employees on information security policies, best practices, and emerging threats. Security awareness programs should be dynamic and tailored to different roles within the organization.
- **Culture of Security:** Foster a culture where security is everyone's responsibility. Encourage employees to be vigilant, report suspicious activities, and actively participate in security initiatives. Recognize and reward good security practices to reinforce positive behavior.

Effective Incident Response and Recovery

- **Preparedness:** Ensure that the organization is well-prepared to respond to security incidents. This includes having a well-defined incident response plan (IRP), conducting regular drills, and ensuring that all stakeholders understand their roles and responsibilities in the event of an incident.
- **Resilience:** Focus on building resilience by implementing business continuity and disaster recovery plans that can be quickly activated in

response to security incidents. This ensures that the organization can continue operating, even in the face of disruptions.

Leveraging Technology and Automation

- **Advanced Security Tools:** Invest in advanced security tools and technologies, such as AI-driven threat detection, automation platforms, and real-time monitoring systems, to enhance the ISMS. These tools can help identify and respond to threats more quickly and accurately.
- **Automation of Routine Tasks:** Automate routine security tasks, such as vulnerability scanning, compliance checks, and log analysis, to free up resources for more strategic security efforts. Automation can also help ensure consistency and reduce the risk of human error.

Collaboration and Information Sharing

- **Internal Collaboration:** Foster collaboration between different departments and teams within the organization, such as IT, security, HR, legal, and operations, to ensure a unified approach to information security.
- **External Partnerships:** Engage in information-sharing initiatives with industry peers, government agencies, and cybersecurity organizations to stay informed about the latest threats and best practices. Collaboration can also provide valuable support during incidents and help improve the overall security posture.

Compliance and Governance

- **Adherence to Standards:** Ensure that the ISMS adheres to relevant industry standards, such as ISO 27001, GDPR, HIPAA, or PCI DSS. Compliance with these standards not only helps mitigate risks but also enhances the organization's reputation and trustworthiness.
- **Governance Framework:** Implement a strong governance framework that defines roles, responsibilities, and accountability for information security across the organization. Regularly review governance practices to ensure they remain effective and aligned with organizational goals.

Measurement and Reporting

- **Key Performance Indicators (KPIs):** Develop and monitor KPIs to measure the effectiveness of the ISMS. These metrics should cover areas such as risk reduction, incident response times, employee awareness, and compliance levels.

- **Regular Reporting:** Provide regular reports to senior management and stakeholders on the status of the ISMS, highlighting achievements, areas of concern, and recommendations for improvement. Transparent reporting helps maintain focus on security and drives continuous improvement.

Conclusion

Maintaining a robust ISMS is an ongoing process that requires commitment, adaptability, and continuous effort. By integrating security into all aspects of the organization, fostering a culture of security awareness, leveraging advanced technologies, and continuously improving security practices, organizations can protect their information assets, meet regulatory requirements, and build trust with customers and stakeholders. A strong ISMS not only safeguards the organization today but also ensures its resilience and success in the face of future challenges.

Appendix A

Glossary of Terms

Below is a glossary of key terms commonly used in the context of Information Security Management Systems (ISMS) and software development. Understanding these terms is crucial for effective communication and implementation of security practices within an organization.

Access Control
The process of limiting access to information or systems to authorized individuals or entities.
Advanced Persistent Threat (APT)
A sophisticated, long-term cyberattack in which an intruder gains unauthorized access to a network and remains undetected for an extended period.
Authentication
The process of verifying the identity of a user, device, or entity before granting access to a system or data.
Authorization
The process of determining what an authenticated user or entity is allowed to do within a system, such as accessing certain data or executing specific functions.
Availability
The assurance that information and systems are accessible to authorized users when needed.
Business Continuity Plan (BCP)
A plan that outlines procedures for maintaining operations or quickly resuming them in the event of a disruption or disaster.
Compliance
The act of adhering to laws, regulations, standards, or policies that apply to an organization's operations and activities.
Confidentiality
The protection of information from unauthorized access or disclosure.
Data Breach
An incident in which sensitive, confidential, or protected information is accessed, disclosed, or stolen by an unauthorized party.

Data Encryption
The process of converting information into a coded format that can only be accessed or decrypted by authorized users with the appropriate key.
Data Minimization
A principle that suggests collecting only the data that is necessary for a specific purpose and retaining it only for as long as needed.
DevSecOps
A methodology that integrates security practices into the DevOps process, ensuring that security is considered at every stage of the software development lifecycle.
Firewall
A network security device or software that monitors and controls incoming and outgoing network traffic based on predetermined security rules.
Incident Response Plan (IRP)
A documented strategy for detecting, responding to, and recovering from security incidents, such as data breaches or cyberattacks.
Information Security Management System (ISMS)
A systematic approach to managing sensitive company information, ensuring its confidentiality, integrity, and availability through a set of policies, procedures, and controls.
Integrity
The assurance that information is accurate, complete, and protected from unauthorized modification or destruction.
Intrusion Detection System (IDS)
A security tool that monitors network or system activities for malicious activities or policy violations and alerts administrators when such activities are detected.
Least Privilege
A security principle that states users should only have the minimum level of access necessary to perform their job functions.
Malware
Malicious software designed to disrupt, damage, or gain unauthorized access to a computer system.
Multi-Factor Authentication (MFA)
A security process that requires users to provide two or more verification factors to gain access to a system, enhancing security beyond just a password.
Penetration Testing (Pen Test)
A simulated cyberattack against a system to identify vulnerabilities that could be exploited by attackers.

Phishing
A fraudulent attempt to obtain sensitive information by pretending to be a trustworthy entity in electronic communications, such as emails or websites.
Privacy by Design
A framework that integrates privacy into the design and operation of systems, processes, and products from the outset.
Risk Assessment
The process of identifying, analyzing, and evaluating risks to information security, followed by determining the appropriate measures to mitigate or manage those risks.
Risk Management
The process of identifying, assessing, and controlling risks to an organization's information assets, including the implementation of security measures to reduce risk to an acceptable level.
Security Information and Event Management (SIEM)
A system that collects, analyzes, and correlates security data from various sources to detect and respond to security incidents.
Software Composition Analysis (SCA)
A process that identifies open-source components in a software project and evaluates them for vulnerabilities, licensing issues, and compliance risks.
Supply Chain Security
The practice of managing and securing the entire supply chain, including third-party vendors and suppliers, to prevent vulnerabilities and threats from compromising an organization's security.
Threat Modeling
A process used to identify, assess, and address potential security threats to a system or application, often during the design and development stages.
Vulnerability
A weakness or flaw in a system, application, or network that can be exploited by attackers to gain unauthorized access or cause damage.
Zero Trust
A security model that assumes no user, device, or application can be trusted by default, and requires continuous verification of identities and access privileges regardless of their location within or outside the network.

This glossary provides a foundational understanding of key terms in information security and software development. It is intended to help stakeholders across the organization communicate more effectively and implement security practices with greater clarity and consistency.

Appendix B

Sample Templates for Risk Assessment and Treatment

This appendix provides sample templates that can be used for conducting risk assessments and creating risk treatment plans within an Information Security Management System (ISMS). These templates are designed to help organizations systematically identify, evaluate, and mitigate risks to their information assets.

Risk Assessment Template

Purpose:
To identify and evaluate risks associated with information assets, and to determine the potential impact and likelihood of those risks materializing.
Instructions:

- Use this template to document identified risks, their potential impacts, and the likelihood of occurrence.
- Assign a risk level based on the combination of impact and likelihood.
- Determine the appropriate controls or actions to mitigate each risk.

Template:

Risk ID	**Asset**	**Threat**	**Vulnerability**	**Impact**	**Likelihood**	**Risk Level**	**Existing Controls**	**Additional Controls Needed**	**Responsible Party**	**Review Date**
001	Customer Data	Unauthorized access	Weak password policy	High	Medium	High	Strong authentication (MFA)	Implement password complexity rules	IT Security Team	01/01/2024
002	Financial Records	Data breach	Outdated software	Critical	High	Critical	Regular software updates	Perform immediate software upgrade	IT Department	01/02/2024
003	Employee	Phishing attack	Lack of employe	Medium	High	High	Phishing awarene	Conduct additio	HR Department	01/03/2024

	Information		e training				ss training	nal phishing simulations		
004	Source Code	Unauthorized modification	Inadequate access controls	High	Low	Medium	Role-based access control	Review access permissions quarterly	Development Team	01/04/2024

Risk Treatment Plan Template

Purpose:
To outline the actions to be taken to mitigate identified risks, including the responsible parties, timelines, and expected outcomes.

Instructions:

- Use this template to document the risk treatment strategies for each identified risk.
- Specify the risk treatment option (e.g., mitigate, transfer, avoid, accept) and the actions required.
- Assign responsibilities and set deadlines for implementing the treatment actions.

Template:

Risk ID	Risk Description	Risk Level	Treatment Option	Treatment Actions	Responsible Party	Deadline	Status
001	Unauthorized access to customer data	High	Mitigate	- Implement password complexity rules - Enforce MFA for all users	IT Security Team	01/10/2024	In Progress
002	Data breach due to outdated software	Critical	Mitigate	- Perform immediate software upgrade - Schedule regular software updates	IT Department	01/15/2024	Planned
003	Phishing attack on employee information	High	Mitigate	- Conduct additional phishing simulations - Increase phishing awareness training	HR Department	01/20/2024	Ongoing
004	Unauthorized modification of source code	Medium	Mitigate	- Review access permissions quarterly - Implement	Development Team	01/25/2024	In Progress

				change management procedures			

Risk Register Template

Purpose:
To maintain a centralized record of all identified risks, their status, and progress on treatment actions. The risk register helps track and manage risks over time.

Instructions:

- Use this template to record and monitor all identified risks, their treatment actions, and the current status.
- Regularly update the register as risks are reassessed, treated, or closed.

Template:

Risk ID	Risk Description	Risk Level	Treatment Actions	Responsible Party	Status	Last Updated	Comments
001	Unauthorized access to customer data	High	- Implement password complexity rules - Enforce MFA for all users	IT Security Team	In Progress	01/05/2024	MFA rollout started
002	Data breach due to outdated software	Critical	- Perform immediate software upgrade - Schedule regular software updates	IT Department	Planned	01/06/2024	Upgrade scheduled
003	Phishing attack on employee information	High	- Conduct additional phishing simulations - Increase phishing awareness training	HR Department	Ongoing	01/07/2024	Next simulation scheduled
004	Unauthorized modification of source code	Medium	- Review access permissions quarterly - Implement change management procedures	Development Team	In Progress	01/08/2024	Permission review completed

Risk Communication Plan Template

Purpose:
To ensure that all stakeholders are informed about identified risks, their potential impact, and the actions being taken to mitigate them.

Instructions:

- Use this template to document how and when information about risks will be communicated to stakeholders.
- Specify the communication channels, frequency, and the responsible party for each communication.

Template:

Communication Activity	**Audience**	**Content**	**Frequency**	**Channel**	**Responsible Party**
Risk Assessment Results	Senior Management	Summary of identified risks and risk levels	Quarterly	Presentation	CISO
Risk Treatment Updates	IT Security Team	Detailed update on ongoing risk treatment actions	Monthly	Email Report	IT Security Manager
Incident Response Review	All Employees	Overview of recent security incidents and lessons learned	After each incident	Town Hall Meeting	HR Department
Compliance Status Report	Regulatory Authorities	Report on compliance with security regulations and standards	Annually	Formal Report	Compliance Officer

These templates provide a structured approach to managing risks within an ISMS. By using these templates, organizations can ensure that risks are systematically identified, assessed, treated, and communicated, thereby strengthening their overall security posture. Regular updates and reviews of these documents are essential for maintaining an effective risk management process.

Appendix C

Additional Resources and Reading

This appendix provides a curated list of additional resources and recommended reading materials that can help deepen your understanding of Information Security Management Systems (ISMS) and related topics in information security and software development. These resources include books, articles, standards, and websites that are valuable for professionals seeking to enhance their knowledge and stay up-to-date with industry best practices.

Articles and Whitepapers

- **"An Introduction to ISO/IEC 27001"** by BSI Group
  This whitepaper provides an overview of ISO 27001, including its key requirements, benefits, and steps for implementation.
- **"The State of DevSecOps"** by GitLab
  An annual report that explores trends, challenges, and best practices in DevSecOps, offering insights into how organizations are integrating security into their development pipelines.
- **"Building a Culture of Security: A Guide for Your Organization"** by SANS Institute
  This article offers practical advice on creating and maintaining a security-first culture within an organization, with a focus on employee engagement and awareness.
- **"Understanding Zero Trust Architecture"** by NIST
  This document provides a detailed explanation of the Zero Trust security model, including its principles, components, and implementation strategies.
- **"Threat Intelligence: What It Is, and How to Use It Effectively"** by Gartner
  This article explains the concept of threat intelligence, its importance in modern cybersecurity, and how organizations can effectively use it to enhance their security posture.

Standards and Frameworks

- **ISO/IEC 27001:2022 – Information Security Management Systems**
  The international standard for information security management, providing requirements for establishing, implementing, maintaining, and continually improving an ISMS.
- **NIST Cybersecurity Framework (CSF)**
  A voluntary framework developed by the National Institute of Standards and Technology (NIST) that provides guidelines for managing and reducing cybersecurity risks.
- **CIS Controls v8**
  A set of best practices and guidelines developed by the Center for Internet Security (CIS) for improving cybersecurity defenses, applicable to organizations of all sizes.
- **OWASP Top Ten**
  A list of the top ten most critical web application security risks, published by the Open Web Application Security Project (OWASP), with guidelines for mitigating these risks.
- **COBIT 2019 – Governance of Enterprise IT**
  A framework for the governance and management of enterprise IT, providing best practices for aligning IT goals with business objectives, including security and risk management.

Websites and Online Resources

- **ISO (International Organization for Standardization)**
  Website: www.iso.org
  Description: The official website of the ISO, where you can find information on ISO standards, including ISO 27001, and purchase official documents.
- **NIST (National Institute of Standards and Technology)**
  Website: www.nist.gov
  Description: A U.S. government agency that develops and promotes measurement standards, including the NIST Cybersecurity Framework and other cybersecurity guidelines.
- **OWASP (Open Web Application Security Project)**
  Website: www.owasp.org
  Description: A nonprofit organization focused on improving software security, providing a wealth of resources, tools, and best practices, including the OWASP Top Ten.

- **CIS (Center for Internet Security)**
  Website: www.cisecurity.org
  Description: An organization that provides best practices, tools, and resources to help organizations improve their cybersecurity posture, including the CIS Controls.
- **SANS Institute**
  Website: www.sans.org
  Description: A leading provider of cybersecurity training, certification, and research, offering a wide range of resources, including whitepapers, articles, and courses.
- **GitLab DevSecOps Resources**
  Website: www.gitlab.com
  Description: A platform that offers resources and tools for integrating security into the DevOps lifecycle, including articles, case studies, and best practices for DevSecOps.
- **BSI Group**
  Website: www.bsigroup.com
  Description: The British Standards Institution (BSI) provides resources, training, and certification services for ISO standards, including ISO 27001.

These resources are intended to support your ongoing learning and implementation of information security best practices within your organization. By staying informed and continually expanding your knowledge, you can better manage the challenges and complexities of maintaining a robust ISMS and securing your software development processes.

About The Author

Mohamed Fawzi Elgendi

Mohamed Fawzi Elgendi is a distinguished Chief Digital and AI Officer, as well as a Chief Information Security Officer (CISO), with over 15 years of experience in the fields of information security, digital innovation, and artificial intelligence. Throughout his career, Mohamed has been a driving force behind transformative technological advancements, consistently pushing the boundaries of what is possible in the digital and AI landscape.

Mohamed's educational background includes a bachelor's degree in computer and systems Engineering and a Post Graduate Program in Artificial Intelligence for Leaders. His extensive knowledge and technical expertise span across software development, IT operations, and advanced AI technologies, making him a versatile leader capable of navigating the complexities of modern digital ecosystems.

In his dual roles, Mohamed has led the integration of security into the heart of digital transformation strategies, ensuring that security is not just a checkbox but a critical enabler of business innovation and growth. He has successfully developed and implemented comprehensive security frameworks that protect organizations from an ever-evolving array of cyber threats, all while fostering a culture of continuous improvement and resilience.

Beyond his professional achievements, Mohamed is the founder of the Fawzooz Initiative, a program dedicated to providing cultural and educational content for youth. This initiative underscores his passion for empowering the next generation with the knowledge and skills they need to thrive in an increasingly digital world.

As a thought leader and advocate for digital excellence, Mohamed frequently shares his insights on the convergence of technology, AI, and security through speaking engagements, writing, and his website, www.fawzooz.ai

His work is driven by the belief that strong digital leadership, combined with robust security practices, is essential for organizations to succeed in today's fast-paced technological environment.

Whether he is spearheading digital innovation or advocating for comprehensive security strategies, Mohamed Fawzi Elgendi is at the forefront of shaping the future of technology and cybersecurity.

www.ingramcontent.com/pod-product-compliance
Ingram Content Group UK Ltd.
Pitfield, Milton Keynes, MK11 3LW, UK
UKHW040228290926
15471UKWH00001B/62

9 789948 702580